CULTURAL

POLITICS

Volume 15, Issue 1
March 2019

CULTURAL
POLITICS

Volume 15, Issue 1
March 2019

QUESTIONING the SUPER-RICH

Special Issue Editors
Jennifer Smith Maguire and Paula Serafini

QUESTIONING the SUPER-RICH

Representations, Structures, Experiences

Paula Serafini and Jennifer Smith Maguire

Abstract The authors outline how multiple dimensions—historical and contemporary; global and local; political, economic, social, and cultural—inform an understanding of the super-rich. Recent super-rich scholarship is reviewed with regard to three themes: discourses and representations; mechanisms and structures; experiences and identities. The empirical and conceptual insights of the contents are then highlighted, with regard to the significance of discourses of legitimacy, namely, those of meritocracy, civility, and luxury; the intersections of race and class that underpin assumptions about and representations of wealth; institutional and political-economic dynamics, in relation to international financial systems and property markets; and experiences and attitudes, examined via elites' professional identities and cultural practices. The authors suggest that questioning the super-rich provides an avenue for the study of power in society, how it is reproduced, and how global hierarchies may be shifting. To that end, the articles attempt to make visible the brute force of the infrastructures (politics and policy, cultural and occupational conventions, financial devices and systems) that are occluded by the tendency to focus on the gloss of super-rich lifestyles; to draw attention to the long-term and newly emerging tensions within and between categories of wealth and of elites, and spheres of political, economic, and cultural activity; and to contribute to an understanding of how the accumulation of wealth is perpetuated and excused through discourses of legitimation, structural dynamics, and lived identities. These are much-needed critical interventions at a time of escalating inequality.

Keywords discourse, elite, identity, representation, super-rich

Cultural Politics, Volume 15, Issue 1, © 2019 Duke University Press
DOI: 10.1215/17432197-7289444

A *Guardian* columnist (Cosslett 2018) recently demanded, "Are we really going to let the super-rich take all the art?" Warning readers about art consultants buying Picassos in bulk and museum collections grinding to a halt as art becomes the best performing asset class of the year, the columnist contemplates a future "in which only the super-rich get to bask in the beauty of humanity's masterpieces" and notes, "I don't especially begrudge them their monopoly on vulgar yachts or tacky hotels, but when they start stealing the art, I'm liable to start rocking back and forth while muttering 'Full communism!' under my breath." The piece makes manifest a range of recurrent anxieties and objections that characterize writings on the super-rich, including the division between a mega wealthy elite and everybody else; changes in global markets and structural factors that enable extreme accumulations of wealth; fears around the loss of culture in the face of sheer economic might; and the assumption that the super-rich are robbing "us," the 99%, of our cultural heritage.

Questioning the super-rich—unpacking the legitimacy of the hyper concentration of wealth, unveiling the financial devices and systems that make it possible, and laying bare its consequences and limitations— could not come at a more timely moment. As in the above example, there is a general sense of the deepening chasm between the very wealthy and "the rest," expressed and reproduced through their seeming monopolization of the good life (and good art). The super-rich appear increasingly isolated in a foreign land in which different tax regimes and life expectancy outcomes apply. And yet, our capacity to grasp the situation is inhibited, in part by the sheer magnitude of the chasm, by the deeply entrenched "wicked problems" bound up

with those inequalities locally and globally, and by the difficulties in gaining an "inside view" of the machinations and mind-sets, infrastructures, and ideologies at work in the perpetuation of the super-rich. As such, attention tends to shift to the surface: the ostentatiousness of super-rich individuals, their lifestyles, and their accoutrements. In turn, what remains hidden from view are the institutional, ideological, and conventional bases on which rest the reproduction of inequality. With this special issue, we suggest that social science has a particularly crucial role to play in enhancing our capacity to grasp and, more so, to challenge the current situation, by bringing to bear a diverse range of theoretical and methodological tools for understanding the *contingent* accomplishment, reproduction, and legitimation of the power relations that sustain and exacerbate the chasm between the super-rich and "the rest."

The global economy has been shaped for more than five decades by the rise of multinational corporations and global brands, escalating outsourcing and offshoring, and the increasing withdrawal of the state from the provision of a social safety net. In the past decade, a protracted economic slowdown and austerity measures have been accompanied by accelerating concentration of wealth in the hands of a few. The statistics on global inequality grow increasingly stark, as marked by Oxfam in successive annual reports on global inequality, suitably timed to coincide with the annual World Economic Forum meeting for global political and business leaders in Davos, Switzerland. A growing popular awareness of and dissatisfaction with global and local inequalities have shaped public views on wealth, luxury, and elites, and given rise to highly visible protest movements. And yet, wealth—and the myth of wealth—continues to work in unintended ways. The cry of "we are the 99%," as espoused by Occupy and other movements for distributive justice, may fuel commitment to the redistribution of economic resources (Chomsky 2012; Piketty 2014; Dorling 2014; Sayer 2015). However, it also invigorates the reproduction of structural inequalities, through the defensive measures of the 1 percent, and the aspirational strategies of those wishing to join it.

At the same time that the gap between the 1 percent and the 99 percent has widened, new groups are ascending into the elite, from both established and emerging economies. In 2016, 55 percent of the world's 2,397 billionaires were entirely "self-made"; 20 percent of those billionaires were from China, Russia, India, and Brazil (Wealth-X 2017). The makeup of the super-rich is rapidly changing as the leading economies of the global South increase their share of the market, shaking the foundations of the West's domination on economic but also cultural terms. This has led to shifting divisions and alliances within and between the upper-middle classes and ascendant ultra-affluent at both local and global scales.

As the mechanisms for the creation and concentration of wealth transform, and global wealth becomes ever more concentrated (Beaverstock, Hubbard, and Short 2004; Di Muzio 2015), the representational politics of status continue to shift (Faiers 2014) between positions of ambivalence. On the one hand, there are demure performances of super-rich status. Following the financial crisis of 2008, newspapers reported on luxury goods shoppers asking for plain shopping bags (Knowledge@Wharton 2009). Similarly, we might look to the consecration of privilege enacted through the discourse of

meritocracy (Littler 2017), as in the case of the current president of the United States, who, despite being born into wealth, presents himself as a self-made man (Serafini 2017). These are poignant examples of the complex structural and representational dynamics of wealth: as the majority make material adjustments in an age of austerity, the super-rich modulate the symbolic language of their wealth. On the other hand, ostentatious performances by the super-rich verge on the carnivalesque: the current president of the United States (again) in his gold-plated elevator (Littler, this issue); a Russian oligarch's £360 million super yacht (Burford 2017); a Chinese tycoon shopping with an entourage of robot handmaidens (Mullin 2016). Such examples sit within a rich vein of popular accounts of the wealthy and their misbehaviors, from F. Scott Fitzgerald's *Great Gatsby* (1925) to Brett Easton Ellis's *American Psycho* (1991) to Kevin Kwan's *Crazy Rich Asians* (2013).

So too do these examples sit within a long tradition of social scientific scholarship on the mentalities and practices of economic elites, from Thorstein Veblen's ([1899] 1994) influential account of the nouveaux riches of the 1890s, to more recent work on the new global power elite, conspicuous philanthrocapitalism, and emerging modes of good taste (e.g., Cassidy 2015; Daloz 2010; Hay and Muller 2013; Featherstone 2014; Schimpfössl 2014; Smith Maguire and Lim 2015). The study of contemporary elites has emerged from a range of disciplinary perspectives and in relation to an array of empirical foci; this has produced complementary if not always intersecting bodies of knowledge with regard to the lived experiences, discourses, and institutional infrastructure of the super-rich (e.g., Freeland 2013; Sayer 2015; Hay and Beaverstock 2016; see

Paula Serafini and Jennifer Smith Maguire

recent special issues assembled by Davis and Williams 2017; Armitage 2018; Cousin, Khan, and Mears 2018). All of this work underlines the contemporary significance of the super-rich. To study economic elites is to study power and inequality from above (Khan 2012).

This special issue thus offers critical reflection on the category of the super-rich. Who are the super-rich? How do they produce and reproduce their status? How are the figures of the super-rich differently configured across time and space? From a range of disciplinary perspectives, the collection of articles utilizes the super-rich as a lens to examine political, economic, and cultural shifts with regard to the aesthetic, spatial, and financial dimensions of wealth and power. Questioning the super-rich, we suggest, provides an avenue for the study of power in society, how it is reproduced, and how global hierarchies may be shifting with the decentering of the West. To that end, the articles attempt to make visible the brute force of the infrastructures (politics and policy, cultural and occupational conventions, financial devices and systems) that are occluded by the tendency to focus on the gloss of super-rich lifestyles; this requires attention to the long-term and newly emerging tensions within and between categories of wealth and of elites, and spheres of political, economic, and cultural activity. Furthermore, the authors contribute to an understanding of how the accumulation of wealth is perpetuated and excused through discourses of legitimation, structural dynamics, and lived identities. These are much-needed critical interventions at a time of escalating inequality when the "parallel country" (Frank 2007) of the super-rich has amassed half of the global wealth.

Super-Rich Scholarship

Studying the super-rich comes with specific challenges, both methodological and disciplinary. Access is often the main barrier in studying the lives of the elites; however, the social science preoccupation with class strictly in terms of disadvantage (e.g., Moore, Gibson, and Lumby 2018) can also pose obstacles, framing the study of elites as a peripheral luxury. However, recent work has compellingly argued that we must not only study the oppressed and the marginalized, but we must also "study up" to fully understand and challenge social and economic inequality (e.g., Di Muzio 2015; Khan 2012). That argument provided the starting point for an event we organized in May 2017 that brought together a range of social science and arts and humanities scholars looking at the super-rich as a serious object of study. Funded by CAMEo, the University of Leicester's Research Institute for Cultural and Media Economies, the symposium brought together several of the authors featured herein, as well as others such as Jonathan Beaverstock, who recounted experiencing journal editors' successive dismissals of the research topic when seeking to publish what has become a seminal article in the field (Beaverstock, Hubbard, and Short 2004). While related scholarship has gathered momentum since that time, the super-rich remain under-researched—hence the contributions in this special issue. Three themes in particular emerge from recent scholarship, which help to frame the intent and content of the special issue: the discourses and representations, mechanisms and structures, and lived experiences and identities of the super-rich.

Discourses and Representations
Studies of the discursive dimensions of the super-rich have explored the ways in which representations of the wealthy are shaped by both celebratory and critical frames, and circulated as part of the flow of information and imagery about class, power, and privilege (Kendall 2011). Historical comparisons have highlighted the continuity of certain narrative constructions of the wealthy, both approving ("rags to riches" stories) and disapproving ("get rich quick" stories), as well as changes, as the justification of wealth has shifted from religious virtue to individual happiness (Fluck 2003). Representations of the super-rich, their lives and excesses, serve to individualize and naturalize inequality, helping to legitimate the structural processes underpinning extreme concentrations of wealth (Jaworski and Thurlow 2017). Representations of wealth symbolically and ideologically work to obscure structural processes that reproduce the advantages of elites, from the transnational movement of capital to urban planning and the organization of credit that enables excessive consumption. This discursive misdirection allows seeming contradictions to pass unnoticed, as when individuals simultaneously hold prowealth attitudes while directing explicit skepticism and criticism at the rich (Horwitz and Dovidio 2017).

Attention has also been directed at the representational practices of the super-rich. These are also marked by continuities and changes over time. If the conspicuous consumption and performances of affluence identified by Veblen ([1899] 1994) have transformed in an era of informationalization when "even billionaires dress casually" (Fluck 2003: 65), they are nevertheless far from extinct. New forms of inconspicuous conspicuousness (Eckhardt, Belk, and Wilson 2014) and elite cultural

capital (Prieur and Savage 2013) continue to symbolically demarcate elites from their aspirants. At the same time, the cultural imaginaries of wealth and power are spectacularly displayed and deployed through material objects, from iconic architecture to luxury retail spaces (e.g., Armitage and Roberts 2016; Crewe and Martin 2016; Sklair and Struna 2013).

Mechanisms and Structures
The mechanisms and structures that enable the hyper concentration of wealth and buttress the reproduction of the super-rich have been the focus of substantial research. These extend from financial instruments to strategies for influencing tax and property policies, which have come to characterize "global" cities like London (Atkinson 2016; Burrows, Webber, and Atkinson 2017). Many such studies emerge from the fields of geography and urban studies, with recurrent themes being the processes and mechanisms that allow for the movement of the super-rich and their capital, and the importance of mobility and the utilization of space.

Special attention has been given to changes in the nature of global capitalism (Haseler 1999), the emergence and intensification of financialization and deregulation, and the ability of the super-rich to better tap into flows of transnational capital so as to increase their own wealth (Irvin 2008; Chesters 2013; Davis and Williams 2017; Volscho and Kelly 2012) through financial products and property (Fernandez, Hofman, and Aalbers 2016). As a result, urban zoning and housing policy are increasingly tailored to the advantage of the super-rich. Certain cities and zones within cities become territories in which the super-rich are embedded spatially and politically, and from which others are excluded. Some of the more structurally oriented work discusses a hegemonic transnational class (see Murray 2015 for a general perspective on this issue, and Kaup 2013 for a look at how this is locally articulated). This kind of work highlights the links between the transnational, mobile lives of those with privilege and the reproduction of a privileged habitus—intersecting with the final theme, below. Overall, this body of work looks to understand the mobilities of the super-rich within a wider global capitalist system that is premised on flow and mobility for the few.

Lived Experiences and Identities
In addition to the more market-based, economic approaches to understanding the structural foundations for the reproduction of the super-rich, work has also been done on the cultural reproduction of the super-rich via particular identities and dispositions, sowed through education and preparation for work (Forbes and Lingard 2015; Tarc and Tarc 2015). A key theme in this regard has been agency, with scholars noting the exaggerated degree of influence and "hyper" agency ascribed to and mobilized by the super-rich (Maclean, Harvey, and Kling 2017). Whether it be in regard to decisions to close themselves off in gated communities (Pow 2011), to engage in charity work or public service (Power et al. 2016; Schimpfössl, this issue), or to partake in research that may actually be critical of them (Gilding 2010), research underlines the super-rich's capacity to choose on their own terms. Agency clearly overlaps with mobility (see Butler and Lees 2006 and Webber and Burrows 2016 on the local impacts of mobility) but also with the performance of everyday life, as studies of the consumption and leisure habits of the super-rich suggest (e.g., Marroun, Wilkinson, and Young 2014; Spence 2014).

Reflecting the peculiar challenges of access associated with studying elites, the lived experiences and identities of the super-rich are often approached indirectly (notable exceptions include Frank [2007] and Greenfield [2017], who offer cultural-anthropological "inside" views of the super-rich, their lifestyles, aspirations, and anxieties). On the one hand, research has examined the mentalities of the super-rich via traces left by their activities and practices. For example, a significant body of work has examined the way in which the super-rich "colonize" space through mechanisms of exclusion and visual territorializing, through the building of gated communities and other exclusive and exclusionary zones (Pow 2011; Knowles 2017; Thurlow and Jaworski 2012). On the other hand, the dispositions of the super-rich are accessed through the frontline service class who are engaged directly with them, such as the intermediaries who manage their financial affairs (Davies 2008) and court high net worth individuals to specific locations as a means to inject capital (Pow 2011, 2017; Atkinson 2016).

The three themes discussed above cover an array of perspectives on the super-rich, from the structural and micro-mechanisms that enable the accumulation and management of wealth, to the discourses that frame wealth, and the subjective experiences of elites. Intersections between these themes highlight both the constitution of the super-rich as a socioeconomic phenomenon and significant research contributions from scholars across the social sciences—many of whom are included in this special issue. The spatial dimensions of the super-rich, for instance, run through examinations of the global distribution of wealth and financial management services, the performance of leisure activities and the symbolic framing of super-rich consumption, and the reverberations of historic East/West divides and Eurocentric perspectives in the contemporary status contests between cadres of elites. Concepts of mobility, agency, legitimacy, inequality, and differentiation have served as critical foci for research and offer potential touchpoints for future cross-disciplinary and cross-cultural insights.

Looking Inside the Super-Rich

The articles in this special issue question the conceptualization of the super-rich from three overarching perspectives. The first several contributions share a concern with critically unpacking key discourses of legitimacy for wealth—namely, those of meritocracy (Littler), civility (Smith Maguire), and luxury (Roberts)—and with troubling the representational conventions of the super-rich (Ojih Odutola, introduced by Frizzell). The next article examines the political-economic and social dynamics of international property markets (Burrows and Knowles). The final two articles turn attention to the experiences and mind-sets of elites, via a focus on their professional identities (Davis) and cultural practices (Schimpfössl).

Jo Littler investigates the way in which elites draw on discourses of meritocracy to validate their position and actions. Littler takes two images as her starting point for a cultural studies–informed deconstruction of the relationship between politics, corporate power, and the media. First: a photo of current US president Donald Trump and former United Kingdom Independence Party leader Nigel Farage standing in Trump's gold-plated elevator; second: a group photo of Trump and Farage joined by a number of men who were instrumental in the Leave.EU campaign (namely, Arron

Banks, Gerry Gunster, Andy Wigmore, and Raheem Kassam). The different layers of the images are considered, from the history of the building where the elevator is located to the relationships between the men photographed and the reactions that the images generated online. Littler points to the contradictory relationship between Trump's flamboyant wealth and his self-positioning as the voice of the masses. She refers to Trump and his ilk as "normcore plutocrats," Littler's term for the ultra-wealthy who "attempt to maintain and increase their power and wealth by performing ordinariness." Littler peels away the mask of ordinariness that these normcore plutocrats put on by means of orchestrated discourse and media texts in their attempts to legitimize their wealth and uphold the myth of meritocracy.

Jennifer Smith Maguire focuses on the nouveau riche faction of the super-rich, arguing that media representations of the nouveaux riches are central in the cultural constitution of the global middle class. She examines the role of a discourse of civility in policing the boundaries of class, often in relation to consumption habits. Smith Maguire identifies three dominant frames in representations of the nouveaux riches aimed at the Western professional middle class: civility, vulgarity, and order (by which groups are positioned and movement between positions is rationalized in relation to both civility and vulgarity). She finds vulgarity to be the most prominent frame, positioning nouveau riche consumption as a crass display of wealth; even if the nouveaux riches know what to buy and where to be seen, they are represented as not knowing how to behave. Nevertheless, some representations in her media sample bestowed the mark of civility, as when nouveau riche behavior and consumption aligned with established Western ideals of bourgeois "good taste." Such representations thus serve to reaffirm the Western upper middle classes' position as gatekeepers of what is and is not civilized. Smith Maguire suggests that the overrepresentation of Asian (particularly Chinese) new rich in the media, and the condescending attitudes toward non-Western rising rich, are manifestations of established upper middle-class anxieties about their place in the global status hierarchy. Connecting representations of the new super-rich to a global socioeconomic climate in flux, Smith Maguire offers a rich account of the way in which the nouveaux riches serve as subjects and symbols of a rapidly changing capitalist system and as anchors for a number of anxieties that result from these transformations.

Joanne Roberts offers a critical examination of the moral position of luxury, painting a picture of imminent crisis both for luxury and for the super-rich in the face of contemporary escalating inequality. Taking a long-term historical perspective, the article provides an overview of the positive and negative conceptualizations and implications of luxury from the classical period to the present. In doing so, Roberts makes clear that the moral position of luxury is both context dependent and bound up with inequality. This sets the foundation for considering the ethical and moral questions that luxury poses to the super-rich, particularly in relation to the tensions between collectivizing redistribution (i.e., taxes) versus individualizing redistribution (i.e., the magnanimity of super-rich philanthropists); between collective luxuries (e.g., high-quality roads, health care, and education) and individual luxuries; and between cultural experiences accessible to the general community versus those reserved for an increasingly removed elite. Roberts

also discusses the relationship between law and morality and references the way in which laws and spaces are increasingly bent to suit the super-rich—from strategies for tax avoidance to the criminalization of rough sleeping—and the dark side to philanthropy, which withholds tax revenue from the state and supplants public expenditure without being democratically accountable.

The special issue then turns to a further account of the super-rich, through the work of artist Toyin Ojih Odutola, insightfully introduced by Deborah Frizzell. Through both images and text, Ojih Odutola constructs a fictional world in which Nigerian noble and mercantile wealth come together. This world is populated with all the expected signifiers of wealth: richly hued and paneled rooms; gilt-framed paintings; red velvet slippers and gold watches; fine fabrics and furs; family estates and equestrian pursuits. At the same time, her works challenge assumptions about wealth through intersections between signifiers of race and class, further complicated by nationality and sexuality—as the marriage that unites the old and new rich Nigerian families is between "the Marquess of UmuEze Amara, TMH Jideofor Emeka, and his husband, Lord Temitope Omodele from the House of Obafemi" (Ojih Odutola 2017). Moreover, as indicated in Frizzell's commentary, Ojih Odutola challenges what wealth means, questioning the equivalences typically drawn between excellence and wealth, and wealth and freedom. She invites us to consider the "beauty and richness in the world" that is flattened by a narrow focus on the economic spoils of affluence, and to challenge the narrow geographical imaginary and normative visual discourse of the cultural imaginary of the super-rich.

Moving away from discourse and representation, Roger Burrows and Caroline Knowles address the financialization of housing in London over the last decade, approaching the subject from the perspective of economic geography. Distinguishing between the "merely wealthy" ("the haves") and the über-wealthy (the "have yachts"), the authors trace the sociospatial transformations of a number of London neighborhoods, through the lived experiences of long-term inhabitants. In their analysis, Burrows and Knowles explore the usefulness of the term *gentrification* for understanding changes in already affluent areas. They question the limits of the frames and methodological tools used for understanding urban transformations and expose the internal stratification of the wealthy. Through rich excerpts from a series of interviews with residents in affluent areas of London, Burrows and Knowles provide an account of the recent stages of an increasing financialization of housing and offer a nuanced perspective on the super-rich by presenting perceptions of this group held by the "merely wealthy."

Aeron Davis explores the structural factors that have shaped the professional identities of contemporary CEOs, whom he regards as primary definers of and influences on contemporary wealth creation. Drawing from interview data, Davis identifies differences in the geographic and social networks, attitudes, and strategies of CEOs, contrasting those located in publicly traded and large, private UK companies. However, he also identifies continuities within this faction, corroborated by data from a demographic audit of CEOs and historical accounts of CEOs going back to the 1970s. These continuities include the professionalization of the CEO occupation, a narrowing of educational

backgrounds and disciplinary expertise and mentalities to the fields of accounting and finance, and a shortening of tenure with an accompanying increased focus on demonstrating performance through short-term profits and share price increases. What emerges is a picture of the "financialized CEO," operating with a foreshortened time horizon and an emphasis on the spectacle of markets (big deals, large-scale restructuring, short-term share movements in funds) to maintain investor interest. Davis demonstrates how these strategies and mind-sets privilege returns for the super-rich investor over long-term innovation and stability for the company, thereby placing financialization and the financialized CEO at the heart of today's extreme wealth and inequality.

Elisabeth Schimpfössl also addresses the lived experiences and identities of the super-rich, through the lens of cultural practice. She explores the charitable and philanthropic practices of Russia's super-rich and discusses the extent to which the frame of philanthrocapitalism is useful for understanding the motivations, dynamics, and relations to the state that lie behind these practices. Through a detailed account of the Russian context and the history of philanthropy in the region, Schimpfössl provides a useful perspective on the cultural practices of the super-rich. More specifically, she provides valuable insights into the identity of Russia's billionaires and their relation to their Soviet upbringing, particularly their often contradictory views on welfare and the state. She suggests that multimillionaire and billionaire philanthropists have constructed distinct ideas about themselves and the role they play in the betterment of Russian society. These ideas help them legitimize their place in the elite.

Concluding Thoughts

The assembled articles contribute to advancing the literature on the super-rich in the three areas identified earlier. The analyses of discourse and representation allow for a more nuanced understanding of the ways in which the super-rich attempt to legitimize their status (Littler) and naturalize luxury and inequality (Roberts). Also highlighted are ways in which representations of and narratives about the super-rich reflect other groups' anxieties about their position in a "Great Chain of Being" (Smith Maguire), and the potential for alternative representations (Ojih Odutola) to disrupt assumptions about wealth (such as those associated with race/ethnicity and nationality) and challenge the historical inequalities on which they rest. Discourses on the super-rich also cut across Burrow and Knowles's analysis of urban transformation, which serves as a window for looking at the super-rich through the eyes of the merely wealthy. The two final articles of the issue explore the lived experiences of the super-rich but return as well to discourses and structural factors. The characteristics of the professional identities and attitudes of the world's top CEOs, as described by Davis, are linked to changes in education and the market, and Schimpfössl ties the philanthropic activities of Russia's super-rich to regional discourses on the role of the state and the duty of individuals.

Studying the super-rich is not only about the super-rich as subjects. The special issue authors invite us to formulate questions about structural issues that the spectacularization of wealth obscures. This includes questioning the distribution of wealth more broadly, the relationship between the public and private sectors, and the politics behind the development of economic and social policy. Studying the super-rich allows us to understand how the accumulation of wealth is perpetuated and excused, but also how middle-class habitus is reproduced, providing an avenue for the study of power in society, and how it is perpetuated. While popular attention has been directed at the new international super-rich and non-Western billionaires becoming more "Westernized," the Western elite are also looking to (some of) the new super-rich, as we see in Mandarin (but not Russian or Arabic) being embedded in (some) elite schools' curricula (Forbes and Lingard 2015). Thus while the middlebrow may resist the super-rich and regard them as vulgar, the old elite seeks to triangulate and benchmark against the distinctive resources of the other, colonizing them to retain the long-standing distance—and thus distinction—that exists between themselves and their newly emerging global competitors.

As a subject, the super-rich are dynamic and constantly evolving, thus inviting further research. While significant research has been done on the mobility, finances, and consumption habits of the super-rich, the representations and representational practices of the super-rich remain under-researched. How do the super-rich make use of different media (e.g., social media, photography, press) to construct their own sense of identity? How are widely distributed images of the super-rich (e.g., Rich Kids of Instagram) referenced by working- and middle-class young people in their own identity-building processes? And how important are images of wealth, luxury, and elite leisure in the building of protest discourse and imaginaries against capitalism and/or the concentration of wealth? Furthermore, while there is extensive work linking the lives of the super-rich with the economic structures in which they are embedded, there is not enough work on the super-rich and their own understandings of wider structural factors (and how these may have enabled their wealth). Another possible future avenue of research is gender. How are images of the worlds of the super-rich gendered? How are gendered hierarchies played out in the world of the super-rich? How are women excluded or co-opted, and how do these dynamics differ for the "new" and "old" super-rich (when billionaires with inherited wealth are far more likely to be women; Wealth-X 2017)? A similar line of inquiry could be followed—as in Ojih Odutola's work—to explore race, ethnicity, and nationality in this context, in terms of both representation and local and transnational constructions of the elites. Thus the special issue invites—if not demands—scholars to undertake further work to question the representations, structures, and experiences of the super-rich; to generate more encompassing, critical accounts of the intended and unintended characteristics and consequences of the super-rich; to further demystify the mechanisms and assumptions that underpin the intensification of the political, economic, and cultural clout of the super-rich; and to fundamentally challenge the increasing isolationism of the super-rich, underlining that when it comes to this planet and our shared future, "they" as much as "we" are the 100 percent.

Acknowledgments

Our thanks to the University of Leicester's Research Institute for Cultural and Media Economies (CAMEo) both for the funding that made the initial research event possible and for research support that assisted with the preparation of this special issue. In particular, our thanks to Isaac Hoff for his invaluable assistance with the survey of existing research on the super-rich.

References

Armitage, John. 2018. "Golden Places, Aesthetic Spaces: An Introduction to the Cultural Politics of Luxury." *Cultural Politics* 14, no. 1: 51–54.

Armitage, John, and Joanne Roberts, eds. 2016. *Critical Luxury Studies: Art, Design, Media.* Edinburgh: Edinburgh University Press.

Atkinson, Rowland. 2016. "Limited Exposure: Social Concealment, Mobility, and Engagement with Public Space by the Super-Rich in London." *Environment and Planning A* 48, no. 7: 1302–17.

Beaverstock, Jonathan V., Philip Hubbard, and John Rennie Short. 2004. "Getting Away with It? Exposing the Geographies of the Super-Rich." *Geoforum* 35, no. 4: 401–7.

Burford, Rachael. 2017. "The Face of Luxury: First Sneak Peek inside Russian Oligarch's £360 Million Super Yacht A Shows Chair in the Shape of a Giant Head." *Daily Mail*, May 6. www.dailymail.co.uk/news/article-4480054/Peak-inside-Russian-oligarch-s-360million-Super-Yacht.html.

Burrows, Roger, Richard Webber, and Rowland Atkinson. 2017. "Welcome to 'Pikettyville'? Mapping London's Alpha Territories." *Sociological Review* 65, no. 2: 184–201.

Butler, Tim, and Loretta Lees. 2006. "Super-Gentrification in Barnsbury, London: Globalization and Gentrifying Global Elites and the Neighbourhood Level." *Transactions* 31, no. 4: 467–87.

Cassidy, John. 2015. "Mark Zuckerberg and the Rise of Philanthrocapitalism." *New Yorker*, December 2. www.newyorker.com/news/john-cassidy/mark-zuckerberg-and-the-rise-of-philanthrocapitalism.

Chesters, Jenny. 2013. "Wealth Inequality and Stratification in the World Capitalist Economy." *Perspectives on Global Development and Technology* 12, nos. 1–2: 246–65.

Chomsky, Noam. 2012. *Occupy.* London: Penguin Books.

Cosslett, Rhiannon Lucy. 2018. "Are We Really Going to Let the Super-Rich Take All the Art?" *Guardian*, March 2. www.theguardian.com/commentisfree/2018/mar/05/are-we-really-going-to-let-the-super-rich-take-all-the-art.

Cousin, Bruno, Shamus Khan, and Ashley Mears. 2018. "Theoretical and Methodological Pathways for Research on Elites." *Socio-Economic Review* 16, no. 2: 225–49.

Crewe, Louise, and Amber Martin. 2016. "Looking at Luxury: Consuming Luxury Fashion in Global Cities." In *Handbook on Wealth and the Super-Rich*, edited by Iain Hay and Jonathan V. Beaverstock, 322–38. Cheltenham, UK: Edward Elgar.

Daloz, Jean Pascal. 2010. *The Sociology of Elite Distinction: From Theoretical to Comparative Perspectives*. Basingstoke, UK: Palgrave.

Davies, James B., ed. 2008. *Personal Wealth from a Global Perspective*. Oxford: Oxford University Press.

Davis, Aeron, and Karel Williams. 2017. "Introduction: Elites and Power after Financialization." *Theory, Culture, and Society* 34, nos. 5–6: 3–26.

Di Muzio, Tim. 2015. *The 1% and the Rest of Us: A Political Economy of Dominant Ownership*. London: Zed Books.

Dorling, Danny. 2014. *Inequality and the 1%*. London: Verso.

Eckhardt, Giana M., Russell W. Belk, and Jonathan A. J. Wilson. 2014. "The Rise of Inconspicuous Consumption." *Journal of Marketing Management* 31, nos. 7–8: 807–26.

Faiers, Jonathan. 2014. "Editorial Introduction." *Luxury* 1, no. 1: 5–13.

Featherstone, Mike. 2014. "Super-Rich Lifestyles." In *Elite Mobilities*, edited by Thomas Birtchnell and Javier Caletrío, 99–135. New York: Routledge.

Fernandez, Rodrigo, Annelore Hofman, and Manuel B. Aalbers. 2016. "London and New York as a Safe Deposit Box for the Transnational Wealth Elite." *Environment and Planning A* 48, no. 12: 2443–61.

Fluck, Winfried. 2003. "What Is So Bad about Being Rich? The Representation of Wealth in American Culture." *Comparative American Studies* 1, no. 1: 53–79.

Forbes, Joanne, and Bob Lingard. 2015. "Assured Optimism in a Scottish Girls School: Habitus and the (Re)Production of Global Privilege." *British Journal of Sociology of Education* 36, no. 1: 116–36.

Freeland, Chrystia. 2013. *Plutocrats: The Rise of the New Global Super-Rich*. New York: Penguin Books.

Frank, Robert. 2007. *Richistan: A Journey through the American Wealth Boom and the Lives of the New Rich*. New York: Random House.

Gilding, Michael. 2010. "Motives of the Rich and Powerful in Doing Interviews with Social Scientists." *International Sociology* 25, no. 6: 755–77.

Greenfield, Lauren. 2017. *Generation Wealth*. New York: Phaidon.

Haseler, Stephen. 1999. *The Super-Rich: The Unjust New World of Global Capitalism*. Basingstoke, UK: Palgrave Macmillan.

Hay, Iain, and Jonathan Beaverstock. 2016. *Handbook on Wealth and the Super-Rich*. Cheltenham, UK: Edward Elgar.

Hay, Iain, and Samantha Muller. 2013. "Questioning Generosity in the Golden Age of Philanthropy: Towards Critical Geographies of Super-Philanthropy." *Progress in Human Geography* 38, no. 5: 635–53.

Horwitz, Suzanne R., and John F. Dovidio. 2017. "The Rich—Love Them or Hate Them? Divergent Implicit and Explicit Attitudes toward the Wealthy." *Group Processes and Intragroup Relations* 20, no. 1: 3-31.

Irvin, George. 2008. *Super Rich: The Rise of Inequality in Britain and the United States*. Cambridge: Polity.

Jaworski, Adam, and Crispin Thurlow. 2017. "Mediatizing the 'Super-Rich': Normalizing Privilege." *Social Semiotics* 27, no. 3: 276–87.

Kaup, Brent Z. 2013. "Transnational Class Formation and Spatialities of Power: The Case of Elite Competition in Bolivia." *Global Networks* 13, no. 1: 101–19.

Kendall, Diana. 2011. *Framing Class: Media Representations of Wealth and Poverty in America*. 2nd ed. Lanham, MD: Rowman and Littlefield.

Khan, Shamus Rahman. 2012. "The Sociology of Elites." *Annual Review of Sociology* 38: 361–77.

Knowledge@Wharton. 2009. "The New High-end Consumer: 'Please Put My Bottega Veneta Wallet in a Plain Bag.'" knowledge.wharton .upenn.edu/article/the-new-high-end-consumer -please-put-my-bottega-veneta-wallet-in-a -plain-bag/.

Knowles, Carol. 2017. "Walking Plutocratic London: Exploring Erotic, Phantasmagoric Mayfair." *Social Semiotics* 27, no. 3: 299–309.

Littler, Jo. 2017. *Against Meritocracy: Culture, Power, and Myths of Mobility.* New York: Routledge.

Maclean, Mairi, Charles Harvey, and Gerhard Kling. 2017. "Elite Business Networks and the Field of Power: A Matter of Class?" *Theory, Culture, and Society* 34, nos. 5–6: 127–51.

Marroun, Sana, Ian Wilkinson, and Louise Young. 2014. "Researching Consumer Behaviour at the Top of the Pyramid: Cultures of Consumption of the Super-Rich." Paper presented at the Australian New Zealand Marketing Academy Annual Conference, Brisbane, December 1–3.

Moore, Tony, Mark Gibson, and Catharine Lumby. 2018. "Recovering the Australian Working Class." In *Considering Class: Theory, Culture, and Media in the Twenty-First Century*, edited by Deirdre O'Neill and Mike Wayne, 217–34. Boston: Brill.

Mullin, Gemma. 2016. "Chinese Tycoon Takes Eight Humanoid Robot Maids Shopping So They Can Carry His Bags." *Mirror,* April 20. www.mirror .co.uk/news/weird-news/chinese-tycoon-takes -8-humanoid-7792679.

Murray, Georgina. 2015. "We Rule the World: An Emerging Global Class Fraction?" *Foresight* 17, no. 2: 208–25.

Ojih Odutola, Toyin. 2017. Artist text for *To Wander Determined.* IFAcontemporary. ifacontemporary .org/unpacking-the-layers-of-toyin-ojih-odutola -to-wander-determined/.

Piketty, Thomas. 2014. *Capital in the Twenty-First Century.* Cambridge, MA: Harvard University Press.

Pow, Choon-Piew. 2011. "Living It Up: Super-Rich Enclave and Transnational Elite Urbanism in Singapore." *Geoforum* 42, no. 3: 382–93.

Pow, Choon-Piew. 2017. "Courting the 'Rich and Restless': Globalisation of Real Estate and the New Spatial Fixities of the Super-Rich in Singapore." *International Journal of Housing Policy* 17, no. 1: 56–74.

Power, Sally, Annabelle Allouch, Phillip Brown, and Gerbrand Tholen. 2016. "Giving Something Back? Sentiments of Privilege and Social Responsibility among Elite Graduates from Britain and France." *International Sociology* 31, no. 3: 305–23.

Prieur, Annick, and Mike Savage. 2013. "Emerging Forms of Cultural Capital." *European Societies* 15, no. 2: 246–67.

Sayer, Andrew. 2015. *Why We Can't Afford the Rich.* Chicago: Policy.

Schimpfössl, Elisabeth. 2014. "Russia's Social Upper Class: From Ostentation to Culturedness." *British Journal of Sociology* 65, no. 1: 63–81.

Serafini, Paula. 2017. "Is It Time for the American Dream to Die?" *The Conversation,* May 10. theconversation.com/is-it-time-for-the-american -dream-to-die-77120.

Sklair, Leslie, and Jason Struna. 2013. "The Icon Project: The Transnational Capitalist Class in Action." *Globalizations* 10, no. 5: 747–63.

Smith Maguire, Jennifer, and Ming Lim. 2015. "Lafite in China: Media Representations of 'Wine Culture' in New Markets." *Journal of Macromarketing* 35, no. 2: 229–42.

Spence, Emma. 2014. "Unravelling the Politics of Super-Rich Mobility: A Study of Crew and Guest on Board Luxury Yachts." *Mobilities* 9, no. 3: 401–13.

Tarc, Paul, and Aparna Mishra Tarc. 2015. "Elite International Schools in the Global South: Transnational Space, Class Relationalities, and the 'Middling' International Schoolteacher." *British Journal of Sociology of Education* 36, no. 1: 34–52.

Thurlow, Crispin, and Adam Jaworski. 2012. "Elite Mobilities: The Semiotic Landscapes of Luxury and Privilege." *Social Semiotics* 22, no. 4: 487–516.

Veblen, Thorstein. (1899) 1994. *The Theory of the Leisure Class.* Mineola, NY: Dover.

Volscho, Thomas W., and Nathan J. Kelly. 2012. "The Rise of the Super Rich: Power Resources, Taxes, Financial Markets, and the Dynamics of the Top One Percent, 1949 to 2008." *American Sociological Review* 77, no. 5: 679–99.

Wealth-X. 2017. *Billionaire Census 2017.* New York: Wealth-X Applied Wealth Intelligence.

Webber, Richard, and Roger Burrows. 2016. "Life in an Alpha Territory: Discontinuity and Conflict in an 'Elite' London Village." *Urban Studies* 53, no. 15: 3139–54.

Paula Serafini is a research associate at CAMEo Research Institute for Cultural and Media Economies, University of Leicester. Her research is on cultural politics, and her interests include cultural production, social movements, art activism, and cultures of extraction in Latin America. Her latest book is *Performance Action: The Politics of Art Activism* (2018).

Jennifer Smith Maguire is professor in the Sheffield Business School, Sheffield Hallam University. Her research focuses on processes of cultural production and consumption in the construction of markets, tastes, and value.

NORMCORE PLUTOCRATS in GOLD ELEVATORS

Reading the Trump Tower Photographs

Jo Littler

Abstract This article analyzes two notorious photos of Donald Trump and Nigel Farage—one on their own, and one alongside Arron Banks, Gerry Gunster, Andy Wigmore, and Raheem Kassam—standing in a gold-plated elevator after Trump had won the US election. The article provides a cultural and political analysis of the plutocrats who are playing at being ordinary "winners," or what it calls normcore plutocrats. Analyzing the symbolic and material contexts of these two images, it considers the physical context of the lift within Trump Tower; the tangled web of relationships uniting the men in the lift; and the first photograph's later life as a social media meme. Asking how a depiction of glittering luxury can be presented as populist revolt, it discusses how elites draw on discourses of meritocracy, of "traveling up the social ladder," to validate their actions. That Trump and friends are not on a ladder but in an express lift symbolizes the attempted velocity of this phase of corporate meritocracy. In the process the analysis provides a multilayered contribution toward understanding how these normcore plutocrats in gold elevators have achieved and extended their power.

Keywords corpocracy, meritocracy, neoliberalism, Trump, Brexit

In November 12, 2016, Donald Trump—whose estimated wealth was at that time around $3.7 billion dollars—was photographed standing in his own glittering, gold-plated elevator after winning the US election on behalf of, he claimed, the forgotten and the left behind (fig. 1). Alongside Trump stood Nigel Farage, former leader of the United Kingdom

Cultural Politics, Volume 15, Issue 1, © 2019 Duke University Press
DOI: 10.1215/17432197-7289458

Independence Party (UKIP), and an instrumental figure in mobilizing the vote for Britain to leave the European Union (or "Brexit"). In the photograph these two portly, besuited white men appear profoundly pleased, with Trump's hand in a thumbs-up pose, Farage grinning open mouthed, his palm gesturing toward Trump as if to say "This guy!" It was taken by Farage's "Brexit buddy" Andy Wigmore, the director of the Leave.EU campaign, who featured in another photograph taken moments afterward alongside more male Brexiteers: Arron Banks, Gerry Gunster, and Raheem Kassam (fig. 2). Both images rapidly achieved notoriety. The image of Trump and Farage quickly traveled from Farage's Twitter feed to the international press, and on to a variety of adapted image afterlives on social media, where it was extensively parodied and achieved widespread notoriety. Novelist Matt Haig (2016), for instance, wrote, "Look at these two young earnest revolutionaries plotting the downfall of the global elite from their humble golden elevator."

The key contradiction that the majority of these comic memes and tweets highlighted was that of, on the one hand, being obviously, flamboyantly, immensely rich, and energetically continuing to increase your personal fortune, while on the other hand purporting to speak for the oppressed masses. Both the image and criticisms of it provoke a crucial question: how has it come to be possible that such incredibly wealthy people are able to pass as representative, as "sticking up for ordinary people," when they're very clearly in a completely different income bracket—in the case of most of them, obscenely wealthy—and are, in fact, actively siphoning off wealth from the rest of the population?

The title of this article indicates that I read these men as "normcore plutocrats," which is a term I developed to describe how sections of the ultra-wealthy attempt to maintain and increase their power and wealth by performing ordinariness (Littler 2018).[1] This article analyzes the cultural politics of these specific normcore plutocrats in relation to these images that frame them. It does so by discussing the material entanglements of these men and their political investments; the multifaceted, gold-plated context of the Trump tower lift; the use of narratives of meritocracy; and the work of these political images in the era of social media reproduction.

In the process it aims to expand the current interest in elites (e.g., Savage and Williams 2008; Davis 2018) by returning to an earlier historical technique in cultural studies and theory of reading the cultural politics of an image in wide circulation. These include, for example, how Roland Barthes read the racialized politics of French nationalism through a *Paris Match* cover, how Stuart Hall read the liberal humanist "social eye" of the magazine *Picture Post*, and how Richard Dyer picked apart the meaning of a photograph of Jane Fonda in relation to the politics of sexuality and peace (Hall 1972; Barthes 1993; Dyer 1979). As Gillian Rose (2012: xvii) put it, "Images are embedded in the social world and are only comprehensible when that embedding is taken into account." This article is influenced by this tradition, returning to its core structural method of picking apart the cultural politics of a media image while at the same time parlaying more recent work on digital image flows, and relating both to the contemporary neoliberal politics of "the corpocracy," in which corporate interests attempt to colonize and dominate the social.

Figure 1 Donald Trump and Nigel Farage at Trump Tower, November 12, 2016.

The Lift in the Tower

The "backdrop" in the Trump Tower photo-graphs is less of a backdrop than a fore-ground. Its gold hues, from ceiling to floor, drip ostentatious wealth, besides which the men joyously position themselves. It radi-ates not only luxury, a continually "animat-ing force of modern capitalism" (Armitage and Roberts 2016: 13), but excessive wealth. As Naomi Klein (2017: 32) so memorably puts it, "The Trump brand stands for wealth itself—or, to put it more crassly, money. That's why its aesthetics are Dynasty-meets-Louis XIV."

Analyzing the material context of the lift itself tells us more about the cultural politics of this moment. It is situated in Trump Tower, which was constructed by Donald Trump on the site of a former department store, Bonwit Teller, after he bought it in 1979. Trump had wanted to own and build on the site for years. Bonwit Teller had a spectacular art deco entrance outside the building with a "stupendously luxurious mix of limestone, bronze,

platinum and hammered aluminium" (Gray 2014). Its fifteen-foot-tall limestone relief panels depicted nude women in art deco style, alongside stained glass and large metal grillwork. The Metropolitan Museum of Art wanted to have them both as significant works of art in its collection, and Trump promised them they could have them. But the museum representative arrived in 1980 at the Bonwit Teller building to find the limestone relief panels had been jackhammered into bits. The large metal grille had been lost, claimed spokesperson "John Barron," a recurring figure who was later revealed (by Trump) to be Trump him-self, posing as his own assistant. "Barron" argued that his "independent valuation" had revealed the artistic pieces to have no merit, and that besides, it would have held up production and cost Trump $500,000 (Gray 2014). The museum, the designer of the grillwork, and numerous cultural commentators condemned the destruction of these artifacts, which made front-page news in 1980 (McFadden 1980a, 1980b). If destroying these artifacts not only indicated Trump's violent disregard for existing cultural institutions and social history, and brazen ability to fake truth, it also demonstrated his fundamental aggression toward anything standing in the way of his plans to construct "his own" luxury aesthetic and expand his own capital.

Most skyscrapers at that time were built with steel. Trump, unusually, chose to use ready-mix concrete; the concrete industry, contrary to its earlier history, had by this time built up a strong union membership (Forty 2012: 227). Large sections of the industry were also controlled by the mafia, which had been subject to a concerted government investigation. Several investigative reporters have repeatedly alleged that Trump, at this time, had close connections with the mafia, and that he met with mob leaders. When workers in the concrete industry went on strike in 1982 over their pay and conditions (as ready-mix set so quickly, unions had a lever for power), the concrete at the Trump Tower construction site kept flowing (Johnston 2016). The building's construction, in other words, facilitated union busting and boosted mob power. Two people also died in separate incidents during its construction, and two hundred undocumented Polish laborers—some of whom actually lived on-site—were paid extremely low wages. A subsequent and extremely long-running lawsuit (during which "John Barron" threatened labor lawyers on the phone) ended in the contractor repaying the workers and, as was later revealed in 2017, Trump being forced to pay out $1.375 million (Bagli 2017).

In his business autobiography *The Art of the Deal*, Trump devotes page after page to Trump Tower. He writes, for instance, about how, in the construction of Trump Tower, he wanted to attract not "the sort of person who inherited money 175 years ago" but "the wealthy Italian with the beautiful wife and the red Ferrari" (Trump 1987: 55–56). It is a particular kind of 1980s dream, of chauvinistic masculinity, new money, and overtly phallic symbolism. In *The Art of the Deal* Trump expresses disdain for co-operative housing and rent controls in New York and writes of how he rejected his father's tips on saving money in construction, instead taking after his mother's sense of showmanship, her "flair for the dramatic and grand" (55–56, 182, 79–80). His continual framing of the tower as "awesome" and as a "great success" for him is childlike and narcissistic in its bragging individualism. All that matters is "winning": showing what a great success your personal brand is, how it is the richest and biggest and best, how an individual has achieved ownership: ownership of money, of power over other people, and particularly over women.

The Trump Tower building is missing several floors. Trump omitted ten floor numbers, fudging the figures with the rationale that some of the ceilings are high (Green 2016). Such a profoundly loose connection with the truth resonates with Trump's subsequent penchant for "alternative facts." The building was constructed at the beginnings of the political experiments with neoliberalism in practice in New York. The city had been known for pursuing social democracy through its services and housing, but in the mid-1970s dramatic and austere cutbacks in federal and state funding, combined with a recession, meant that New York nearly became bankrupt (Harvey 2007: 45–47). As Naomi Klein (2017: 142) puts it, this crisis was used to push through a "shock doctrine" expanding corporate power: "Under cover of crisis came a wave of brutal austerity, sweetheart deals to the rich, and privatizations." Dramatic underfunding and deregulation was used to push through tax breaks for corporations and increase corporate power at the expense of citizens. Trump worked with his close friends in powerful positions to extract outlandishly favorable terms for the purchase of Trump Tower. With a $9.5 million down payment, he would sell it for a dollar to the Urban Development Corporation, who would in turn lease it back to him for four decades at an extremely low rate. It is estimated that this tax break windfall was worth $360 million by 2017 (Klein 2017: 142).

The phenomenally favorable terms of the deal (to Trump) was in part permitted because a section of Trump Tower provides privately owned "public space" (POPUS): it includes shops and flats as well as Trump's own offices and apartments. In this sense it is connected to a wider trend in the expansion of privatized "public" space: space that is ostensibly public but owned and controlled by private interests, which geographers including Saskia Sassen, David Harvey, and Doreen Massey have warned about for decades (Sassen 2015; Harvey 2013; Massey 2007). To make this understandable, people can enter as consumers to shop, but any noisy protest against Trump is not acceptable, and protestors have been blocked by security and police (Gabbat 2017).[2]

After Trump's election, a C-Span TV channel was used to screen events in the lobby, showing meetings and "significant" people entering and leaving the "White House North," so named in part because of Donald and Melania Trump's apparent reluctance to leave it, postinauguration, to live in Washington, DC. After the election, the foyer became a privatized, wealth-flaunting media space in which the emergent celebrity presidency was to be staged. The most notorious example was when pop star Kanye West, widely known to be suffering from mental health problems, and who had struggled with opioid addiction, turned up to visit Trump. As Ta-Nehisi Coates (2018) diagnoses in his astute essay linking Kanye, the destructive individualism of celebrity, and internalized racism, "It was a drugged-out West who appeared in that lobby, dead-eyed and blond-haired," desperately seeking the "free" white power that Trump appeared to represent.

The Men in the Photograph

Both the image of Trump and Farage, and the photograph of Trump, Farage, Banks, Gunster, Kassam, and Wigmore taken shortly after it, indicate the tangled web of relationships between corporate and media capital; between the alt-right social media site Breitbart, pollsters Goddard Gunster, and the data-mining marketeers Cambridge Analytica; and between Trump's celebrity and the businessmen who wanted Britain out of the EU so it could be used as a deregulated site for corporate exploitation and as a tax haven. The men in the lift are united by a drive to supremacism. They seek to bolster their own financial and social power through a range of financial, cultural, and technological strategies—including lying—while repeatedly belittling and endangering the less privileged, and the environment, to secure and expand their own resources.

Let us examine these claims in relation to the second photo, which depicts a variety of men instrumental in the Leave.EU campaign. Standing on the other side of Donald Trump is Arron Banks, the UKIP donor who largely bankrolled the Leave.EU campaign. To the left of him is Gerry Gunster, the American pollster who helped win it. Andy Wigmore, the communications director of Leave.EU, has one arm around Nigel Farage, and another around Raheem Kassam, the editor-in-chief of *Breitbart News London* as well as a former UKIP leadership candidate and adviser to Farage. Together they have used chaos and strategy, and strategic chaos, to extend and deepen right-wing political power (Grossberg 2018).

It is possible to tell many stories about the men in this image. One is that they embody the rise of financialization. Arron Banks amassed his fortune working in the financial sector, including at the insurance marketplace Lloyd's of London, and has set up thirty-seven companies, many of which sell or have sold insurance, using variations of his name. In 2017 his wealth was estimated at £250 million (*Economist* 2017). Nigel Farage worked as a commodities trader in London. Raheem Kassam briefly worked for the financial services and investment bank Lehman Brothers before it went bankrupt. Both Farage and Banks have affluent, private-school backgrounds, though neither are as wealthy as Trump, who was given millions by his father, the real estate mogul Fred Trump. Financialization has involved an increase in gambling and speculation on financial trading, and is an industry that has lobbied for looser regulations on commercial companies and less public sector spending and security. It has ascended over the past few decades alongside and in fusion with an aggressive corporate culture that promotes a *rentier* economy (in which income like rent, interest, or capital gains is garnered from preexisting assets) and asset stripping—landing in institutions, selling off assets, and moving on to the next company (Sayer 2016; Lapavitsas 2013; Piketty 2014; Meek 2014). It is perhaps not completely unrelated that Arron Banks was once expelled for stripping out and selling the lead from the roof of his boarding school (Fletcher 2016).

Of course, as any critical theorist knows, what is left out of the picture is just as important as what is in it. A key figure not in the picture but uniting all of them is Robert Mercer, a former computer scientist who gained his wealth through hedge funds and donated generously to both Trump and Farage. Mercer gave Farage the services of Cambridge Analytica, which harvested Facebook data from over 50 million people without their realizing it, and he also campaigned for *Breitbart*'s Steve Bannon to take a prominent role in the White House. Analytica's managing director and chief executive were later exposed and filmed in an undercover Channel 4 news operation boasting of manipulating voters, buying candidates, and creating fake information on websites in democracies throughout the world (Channel 4 News 2018). The traffic between the UK and the US mainstream/renegade political right wing and the forms of expertise they lend and trade each other radiate out of both images, not least in the lapel pin Farage wears, where a Union Jack and Stars and Stripes flags are intertwined. The firm Gerry Gunster runs, Goddard Gunster, was paid by Arron Banks to run the Leave.EU campaign. Goddard Gunster specializes in referendums (claiming "a 90% success rate"), having defeated proposals for a tax on large sugary drinks in New York and deposits on plastic bottles; in other words, specifically campaigning against measures to tackle environmental degradation and obesity. The firm also worked for Boris Yeltsin in the 1990s for his political and economic reforms (Reuters 2015), which instigated mass privatization and enabled Russian oligarchs to vastly expand their wealth (Klein 2007: 218–62). By May 2018 Leave.EU had been fined by the UK Electoral Commission, and its chief executive reported to the police, for breaking multiple counts of electoral law during the EU referendum (Weaver and Waterson 2018). The picture of these men together is a testament to this intertwined nexus of capital; political, digital, and media power; and corruption.

An important component of this nexus interconnecting the men in the lift is their relationship to imperialism and racism. Donald Trump's political pronouncements and behavior, while erratic, have notoriously supported the racist views of the "alt-right." He has called Mexicans rapists and promised that he will build a wall between the United States and Mexico. Such racism is built out of white North American imperial superiority over the rest of the Americas. Its overt imperialism was echoed, in a different register, by many of the leading proponents of Brexit. In the Leave.EU campaign, a similarly reactionary imperialist nostalgia—what Paul Gilroy (2004) accurately termed over a decade ago "postcolonial melancholia"—was energized and vitalized through pronouncements that Brexit would make Britain great again. Notably, many of the Brexit boys had expat childhoods: Arron Banks's father made his money through the residues of imperialism, working on a variety of sugar estates across several African countries, including Kenya and Somalia; Banks himself has invested in South African diamond mines (Fletcher 2016). The political framing of their Leave.EU campaign for Brexit was wrapped in overt nationalism, perpetuating and reactivating a muscular love for "imperial greatness." As Gary Younge (2018) put it, Brexit was produced by Britain's delusions of its colonial role: "Our colonial past, and the inability to come to terms with its demise, gave many the impression that we are far bigger, stronger and more influential than we really are."

The presence of Raheem Kassam in this context, alongside men well known for endorsing racist groups and sentiments, stands out, for his is the only nonwhite face. Kassam, a Londoner and an atheist, was a member of the Conservative Party who flirted with the far-right anti-Islam group Pegida before arriving in UKIP. Kassam takes part in a pattern whereby a handful of nonwhite UKIP members are foregrounded to try to show "antiracist" nationalistic credentials. He currently appears on his Twitter feed wearing a suit made of Union Jack fabric. In interviews he talks—using the same trope that people from the center to the right of the political spectrum have deployed for a long time—about being "beyond ideology" (Hayward 2016; Littler 2017). Nationalist right-wing politics is fused with a sense of breaking beyond the norm, of shattering the normal rules of the political game; it participates in a fantasy that they are beyond ideology, and, like trolling, that it is just a game of poking the powerful, where ethics and feelings don't matter (Phillips 2016; Littler 2018). Kassam's career took off when he started supporting extreme immigration controls and making spectacular statements against Islam and Palestine (Walker 2016). This projection of "difference" and antipolitics (Glaser 2018) has been key to the "offer" of Brexit and Trump. The people in the lift, to borrow the title of Aeron Davis's book, are reckless opportunists (2018); they reject "the establishment" and pander to people's feelings of rejection in the interests of their own massive material gain and self-promotion.

What also unites these men, besides their love of far-right politics and corporate power, is their gender—it is, after all, only men in the lift—and the specific mode of their masculinity. Andy Wigmore, the communications director of Leave.EU, took the Trump and Farage photo and

Figure 2 Gerry Gunster, Arron Banks, Donald Trump, Nigel Farage, Andy Wigmore, and Raheem Kassam at Trump Tower, November 12, 2016.

appears in the second photo. Wigmore likes to describe this gang on social media as "the bad boys of Brexit" and "The Brex Pistols."[3] Such self-styling attempts to capture something of the symbolism of punk and of renegade outlaws for wealthy white middle-aged men. It carries with it more than a whiff of "the new lad": of ostensibly joking around when styling themselves as renegade and hedonistic, compacting themselves together in a tightly knit brotherhood of masculinity and repeated misogyny, seeking to restore a lost masculine power through aggressive talk toward women. The idea that we are "postracism" or "postfeminism," so endemic in the 1990s and 2000s, was shattered as increased votes for Trump and UKIP activated and reactivated racism, xenophobia, and sexism, with all the destructive and vicious power that these entailed (Hochschild 2016). Raheem Kassam posted a now-deleted tweet in June 2016 suggesting that the first minister of Scotland, Nicola Sturgeon, should have "her mouth taped up. And her legs, so she can't reproduce" (Oppenheim 2016).

An elevator is an enclosed space. Donald Trump has notoriously been accused of sexual harassment by more

than a dozen women (Gray 2017). One such woman was Stacia Robataille (2017), who a year after this photo was taken, tweeted, "I was once on an elevator alone with @realDonaldTrump (and a man w/ him) at Madison Square Gardens. He was aggressive & told me I was coming home with him. I laughed, stating I was married to a Ranger. He guaranteed me my husband didn't make as much money as him." The aggressive assumptions of, first, ownership of women and, second, that a woman he wanted would simply become sexually aroused by the mere mention of his earning more money than her husband (a wealthy hockey star) stands out in this account. It foregrounds a patently misogynistic and mercenary value system. It recalls the notorious leaked recording from 2005 in which Trump was heard bragging to Billy Bush of grabbing women "by the pussy." Proposing that women "love it," he was not at all ashamed of, but rather actively endorsing, such behavior; even if the celebration itself was under the radar and the recording was secret, it was laddishly explained away by his publicists as "locker-room banter" (*New York Times* 2016). Like so many of these actions, it is not generally acceptable, but his behavior works to attempt to *make* it so, to shift the codes of normality and the norms of acceptability to the right.

The Lift Not the Ladder: Hypermeritocracy

We use cultural stories to narrate our lives: of what is ordinary, of how people do and should live. One of these is the story that says people need to be given the chance to work hard to activate their talent to rise up and climb the ladder of success. This is the narrative of meritocracy, which has been used as a key cultural means of legitimation for contemporary capitalism—a neoliberal narrative that promises opportunity while creating new forms of social division (Littler 2018).

Such narratives of neoliberal meritocracy are implicitly at work here, in the affective registers; they look surprised and ecstatic to be here, not statesmanlike. Their deportment says, These guys made it! The ordinary blokes made it not just up the ladder but into the gold-plated lift! The garnering of such extreme plutocratic wealth is what Thomas Piketty (2014: 265) calls "hypermeritocracy." The vast majority of these men were extremely wealthy to begin with, and all of them gained their money through forms of exploitation. But the lift photo presents them as lads who have made it and who are enjoying a good time.

We might read their expressions as saying, We weren't supposed to be here!—in these positions of political power. They are not supposed to be there in more ways than one. They aren't supposed to be there because they are not actually dealing with the issues they purport to be (such as helping the National Health Service [NHS]) despite ventriloquizing them: in fact the contrary, as their

actual policies (e.g., privatization) break the pledges they stand for.[4] They also aren't supposed to be there because decades of technocratic neoliberalism, in which political machines become more divorced from the grassroots via "partyless democracy" and "postdemocracy," have seen candidates parachute into roles by a managerial center of political machinery (Mair 2000; Crouch 2004). It is the slippage between these reasons that they weren't supposed to be there that *enables* them to be there. Farage and Trump have notoriously framed themselves as breaking with the elitism of an existing liberal settlement, with the status quo. To do this they have used racism, xenophobia, and sexism to "say the unsayable," to appear that they are breaking the smooth surface of party politics and offering a radical change and actual power. Voting for them parlayed desires from people left behind through years of neoliberal economic precarity; areas that voted for Brexit, for instance, are also projected to be the areas with the most to lose from it. Voters often talked of wanting "something different" to happen, which UKIP seemed to offer (Barnett 2017). There were pronounced commonalities as well as differences between the reasons for Brexit and the result of the 2016 US election; the most enthusiastic Trump supporters came from wealthy white people, and the largest proportion of pro-Brexit voters were white, affluent voters from southern England (Ashcroft 2016). Even though the white working-class vote was higher for Trump than Clinton, the overall number of working-class voters fell (Grossberg 2018). This is indicative of the extent to which Hillary Clinton was synonymous with a neoliberal status quo since the 1980s, in which US production has been decimated and living standards for the working and lower middle classes have markedly fallen (Younge 2018). Similarly, the working-class leave vote in the United Kingdom was high, although not as high as among the affluent (Ashcroft 2016; Barnett 2017; Dorling, Stuart, and Stubbs 2016).

The cultural pull of contemporary meritocratic discourse is one explanation of why we are in the political grip of these brutal billionaires. As I have explored elsewhere (Littler 2018), these incredibly wealthy men present themselves as everyday, as normcore, and as deserved achievers or meritocrats, in a number of affective ways. Despite being members of an extremely rich elite, they continually frame themselves as hardworking and savvy, projecting images of being deserving toilers, in the process extrapolating a whiff of working-class culture and sticking this onto their overprivileged selves. Farage and Trump have placed themselves and their parties in the rhetorical position of the exploited, stoking hatred toward "elites" and immigrants in the process (Frank 2012: 44). Trump literally broke the established art deco design cultural capital of the Bonwit Teller grillwork, replacing it with shiny glass and gold that connoted new money.

Trump's projection of himself as a brand becomes positioned as a skill to admire in an era when, as Alison Hearn (2016: 656) points out, "most people must now assiduously self-promote and hustle in order to find or protect their jobs"; it becomes "all the qualification he needs to become president." This means that, as Naomi Klein (2017: 33) argues, scandals aren't sticking to Trump because "he didn't just enter politics as a so-called outsider, but somebody who doesn't play by the rules. He entered politics playing by a completely different set of rules—the rules of branding. According to these rules,

you don't need to be objectively good or decent." The entrepreneurial self-branding combines with what Wendy Brown (2018: 15) calls the "libertarian authoritarianism" of Trump: the wild and aggressive Frankenstein monster spawned by neoliberalism promoting aggressive nationalism and corporate marketization. This sedimented logic is what is "made" when Trump and Farage present the image of having "made it."

The Image and Its Afterlives

The images are not selfies or "groupies"; there is no besuited arm bending out to the camera from the group. But neither are they institutional or professionally produced shots. They are personal photography: they are of a genre that connotes close relationships and emotional moments. Trump has his thumbs-up in both photos; he does not wear a tie. These are friends in the lift, sharing their glee, presenting their togetherness, their winning moment against a symbolic backdrop of glittering gold. The private-public nature of the image is accentuated by its being initially shared on social media, as part of Farage's Twitter feed. In an era of "ubiquitous photography," we are surrounded by what Martin Hand (2012: 1) calls "the visual publicization of ordinary life in a ubiquitous photoscape." Both images work by generating the sense that they are part of such "ordinary" ubiquity, just as celebrities generate a sense of ordinary intimacy through their Twitter and Instagram feeds. When anyone can be what Terri Senft (2008) calls a "microcelebrity," the larger celebrity using social media imaging is simultaneously rendered "ordinary" and intimate through it. Trump and Farage use these technologies with bombastic effectiveness.

These images are then "networked

within a range of globally connected flows of communication" (Hand 2012: 1), but they also have a privileged status within these networks. By virtue of the political and celebrity status of who is depicted in and who is posting the images, the photos obviously become of considerable public interest. The photograph marks the other men's proximity to the new center of power that is President Donald Trump, proves their political proximity to him, and attempts to mediate what Trump will "be like" as president to the world. Farage wrote below the image: "It was a great honour to spend time with @realDonald Trump. He was relaxed and full of good ideas. I'm confident he will be a good President." Their manipulation of the image and its materiality and meaning extends to purporting their own compassion: Andy Wigmore pronounced in an interview that he had donated his half of the profits from the Trump and Farage photo sales to the Royal Commonwealth Society (Cooper 2016), again reinforcing the attempt to elide "greatness" with imperialism.

These images of normcore plutocrats are therefore used to attempt to accrue more cultural power in what is now a "fragmented, deregulated, interactive and increasingly factionalized mediascape" (Ouellette and Banet-Weiser 2018: 4). The use of "ordinary" and "direct" social media channels, a personalized message from Farage, and the trappings of a family snap frames these plutocrats as everyday beings who are surprised to inhabit such splendor. The affective awkwardness works by inviting its viewer, who is quite likely not to inhabit such wealth, into seeing that it might be possible for sites of power and privilege to be occupied by people who don't seem "used to it"; their awkwardness and informal glee displace the actual fact of the subjects' vast financial

privileges. This is a populist invitation. As Paolo Gerbaudo (2018) notes, there is an "elective affinity between populism and social media," an affinity mobilized by both right and left, to reactionary and progressive ends. The dominance of corporate media monopolies and the failure to regulate them are a key reason for the rise and expansion of the power of right-wing populism (Fuchs 2018: 9).

Yet the image was also widely parodied and mocked. It was ridiculed through captions. "Trump and Farage in a gold elevator. Laughing. At You," wrote @isolatedBrit (2017). "Men of the people Nigel Farage and Donald Trump pose in golden elevator. Take that, global elites!," lambasted an article in the digital media/marketing industry website *Mashable* (Wagstaff 2016), a sentiment repeated with slight modifications in a wide range of similar tweets. And its visual and material excess was scorned by identifying what it shared with the fascist aesthetic of Adolf Hitler and the Third Reich. The author Robert Harris (2016) tweeted an image of Hitler's golden elevator the subsequent day, a tweet that was shared 3,900 times, with the caption "This was Hitler's elevator at the Berghof to the Eagle's Nest. Just saying." The work of rejecting, belittling, explaining, and lambasting the image is simultaneously but one, and one significant, part of an oppositional and alternative politics.

The photographs in the elevator at Trump Tower propose flamboyant material wealth of corporate plutocrats as the ultimate triumph and show how social and cultural codes of ordinariness have been used and abused to achieve it. Borrowing from social media's tropes of everyday microcelebrity, and blending them into a spectacle of startling success, the image frames this story as one that is not so much about climbing the social ladder to the top as taking a privatized gilt-encrusted express lift. In the process the inequalities that narratives of meritocracy obscure, through their cultural codes of "everyone having the opportunity to make it, if only they try hard enough," are spectacularly elided to a far greater extent than in living memory. The material history of the lift itself—built through the exploited labor of workmen, built on a site in which two people died in construction, built through the corporate leverage of money from public funds, coded as public space policed by the private realm—reveals so much about the value system of the men contained in it. The image signifies and materializes a power grab: of visual time, of material resources, of people's labor and lives and futures; and the men in the lift are laughing at the audacity of having pulled this feat off, so far.

Notes

1. Of course, the super-rich presenting themselves as "normal" also has a longer history, as I discuss elsewhere (Littler 2018).
2. One man, Jeff Bergman, does, however, protest weekly inside Trump Tower in modest and acceptable fashion by reading aloud literature, speeches, and editorials (Helmore 2017).
3. Wigmore has a more elusive background than the others, although it is widely reported that he has won medals for shooting and has represented Belize in sporting competitions.
4. Leave.EU deployed a large red promotional "Brexit bus," stating, for example, that £350 million of extra money would go to the NHS if Britain left the EU. The figure that the United Kingdom pays to the EU after rebates is around half of this; the cost of Brexit is vast (their political rivals suggest £500 million per week), although its very unknowability allows such claims to be made. Crucially, those involved in Leave.EU are of the political tendency that urges privatization of the NHS.

References

Armitage, John, and Joanne Roberts. 2016. "The Spirit of Luxury." *Cultural Politics* 12, no. 1: 1–22.

Ashcroft, Lord. 2016. "How Britain Voted on Thursday, and Why." Lord Ashcroft Polls, June 26. lordashcroftpolls.com/2016/06/how-the -united-kingdom-voted-and-why/.

Bagli, Charles. 2017. "Trump Paid over $1 Million in Labor Settlement, Documents Reveal." *New York Times*, November 28.

Barnett, Anthony. 2017. *The Lure of Greatness: England's Brexit and America's Trump*. London: Unbound.

Barthes, Roland. 1993. *Mythologies*. London: Vintage.

Brown, Wendy. 2018. "Where the Fires Are: Wendy Brown Talks to Jo Littler." *Soundings*, no. 68: 14–25.

Channel 4 News. 2018. "Revealed: Trump's Election Consultants Filmed Saying They Use Bribes and Sex Workers to Entrap Politicians." March 19. www.channel4.com/news/cambridge-analytica -revealed-trumps-election-consultants-filmed -saying-they-use-bribes-and-sex-workers-to -entrap-politicians-investigation.

Coates, Ta-Nehisi. 2018. "I'm Not Black, I'm Kanye." *Atlantic*, May 7. www.theatlantic.com /entertainment/archive/2018/05/im-not-black -im-kanye/559763/.

Cooper, Marta. 2016. "That Photograph of Nigel Farage and Donald Trump in a Lurid Gold Doorway Is Raising Thousands for Charity." *Quartz*, November 24. qz.com/845722/that -picture-of-nigel-farage-and-donald-trump-in -the-gold-doorway-is-raising-thousands-for -charity/.

Crouch, Colin. 2004. *Post Democracy*. Cambridge: Polity.

Davis, Aeron. 2018. *Reckless Opportunists: Elites at the End of the Establishment*. Manchester, UK: Manchester University Press.

Dorling, Danny, Ben Stuart, and Joshua Stubbs. 2016. "Don't Mention This around the Christmas Table: Brexit, Inequality, and the Demographic Divide." *LSE Blogs*, December 21. blogs.lse.ac.uk /europpblog/2016/12/21/christmas-table-brexit -inequality-demographic-divide/.

Dyer, Richard. 1979. *Stars*. London: British Film Institute.

Economist. 2017. "Arron Banks, Bankroller of Brexit, Faces Investigation over His Donations." November 2. www.economist.com/news /britain/21730890-claims-russian-influence -are-complete-bollocks-he-insists-arron-banks -bankroller-brexit.

Fletcher, Martin. 2016. "Arron Banks: The Man Who Bought Brexit." *New Statesman*, October 13. www.newstatesman.com/politics/uk/2016/10 /arron-banks-man-who-bought-brexit.

Forty, Adrian. 2012. *Concrete and Culture: A Material History.* London: Reaktion.

Frank, Thomas. 2012. *Pity the Billionaire: The Hard-Times Swindle and the Unlikely Comeback of the Right.* New York: Picador.

Fuchs, Christian. 2018. "Authoritarian Capitalism, Authoritarian Movements, and Authoritarian Communication." *Media, Culture, and Society* 40, no 5: 779–91.

Gabbat, Adam. 2017. "President's First Trump Tower Homecoming Met with Mass Protest." *Guardian*, August 15. www.theguardian.com/us-news /2017/aug/14/donald-trump-trump-tower -protest-charlottesville.

Gerbaudo, Paolo. 2018. "Social Media and Populism: An Elective Affinity." *Media, Culture, and Society* 40, no 5: 745–53.

Gilroy, Paul. 2004. *After Empire: Melancholia or Convivial Culture?* London: Routledge.

Glaser, Eliane. 2018. *Anti-politics: On the Demonization of Ideology, Authority, and the State.* London: Repeater Books.

Green, Damien. 2016. "Trump Tower Is Actually Ten Floors Shorter than Donald Trump Says It Is." *UK Business Insider*, October 25. uk.businessinsider .com/trump-tower-is-not-as-tall-as-trump-says -2016-10.

Gray, Christopher. 2014. "The Store That Slipped through the Cracks." *New York Times*, October 3.

Gray, Sarah. 2017. "Hockey Star's Wife Describes Meeting an 'Aggressive' Donald Trump in an Elevator." *Fortune*, December 13. fortune.com /2017/12/13/luc-robitaille-wife-experience -aggressive-donald-trump/.

Grossberg, Lawrence. 2018. *Under the Cover of Chaos: Trump and the Battle for the American Right.* London: Pluto.

Haig, Matt (@matthaig1). 2016. "Look at these two young earnest revolutionaries plotting the downfall of the global elite from their humble golden elevator." Twitter, November 13, 2:23 a.m. twitter.com/matthaig1/status /797716382741917696.

Hall, Stuart. 1972. "The Social Eye of Picture Post." *Working Papers in Cultural Studies*, no. 2: 71–120.

Hand, Martin. 2012. *Ubiquitous Photography.* Cambridge: Polity.

Harris, Robert (@Robert___Harris). 2016. "This was Hitler's elevator at the Berghof to the Eagle's Nest. Just saying." Twitter, November 13, 2:21 a.m. twitter.com/robert___harris /status/797746248837107712.

Hayward, John. 2016. "Raheem Kassam: Steve Bannon Is the Man Who Flew to London to Hire This Brown Guy from a Muslim Family." *Brietbart*, November 17. www.breitbart.com/radio/2016 /11/17/raheem-kassam-steve-bannon-man-flew -london-hire-brown-guy-muslim-family/.

Harvey, David. 2007. *A Brief History of Neoliberalism.* Oxford: Oxford University Press.

Harvey, David. 2013. *Rebel Cities.* London: Verso.

Hearn, Alison. 2016. "Trump's Reality Hustle." *Television and New Media* 17, no. 7: 656–59.

Helmore, Edward. 2017. "Read It and Weep: Meet the Man Waging a Weekly Protest at Trump Tower." *Guardian*, December 23. www.theguardian.com /us-news/2017/dec/23/read-it-and-weep-meet -the-man-waging-a-weekly-protest-at-trump -tower.

Hochschild, Arlie. 2016. *Strangers in Their Own Land: Anger and Mourning on the American Right.* New York: New Press.

@isolatedBrit. 2017. "Trump and Farage in a gold elevator. Laughing. At You." Twitter, January 10. Tweet since removed.

Johnston, David Cay. 2016. "Just What Were Donald Trump's Ties to the Mob?" *Politico*, May 22. www .politico.com/magazine/story/2016/05/donald -trump-2016-mob-organized-crime-213910.

Klein, Naomi. 2007. *The Shock Doctrine: The Rise of Disaster Capitalism.* London: Penguin.

Klein, Naomi. 2017. *No Is Not Enough: Defeating the New Shock Politics.* London: Allen Lane.

Lapavitsas, Costas. 2013. *Profiting without Producing: How Finance Exploits Us All.* London: Verso.

Littler, Jo. 2017. "Ideology." In *Keywords for Media Studies*, edited by Jonathan Gray and Laurie Ouellette, 98–101. New York: New York University Press.

Littler, Jo. 2018. *Against Meritocracy: Culture, Power, and Myths of Mobility*. London: Routledge.

McFadden, Robert D. 1980a. "Designer Astonished by Loss of Bonwit Grillwork." *New York Times*, June 8.

McFadden, Robert D. 1980b. "Developer Scraps Bonwit Sculptures; Builder Orders Bonwit Art Deco Sculptures Destroyed." *New York Times*, June 6.

Mair, Peter. 2000. "Partyless Democracy: Solving the Paradox of New Labour." *New Left Review*, no. 2: 21–35.

Massey, Doreen. 2007. *World City*. Cambridge: Polity.

Meek, James. 2014. *Private Island: Why Britain Now Belongs to Someone Else*. London: Verso.

New York Times. 2016. "Transcript: Donald Trump's Taped Comments about Women." October 8. www.nytimes.com/2016/10/08/us/donald-trump-tape-transcript.html.

Oppenheim, Maya. 2016. "Who's in Nigel Farage's Gold Brexit Gang Photo with Donald Trump?" *Independent*, November 14. www.independent.co.uk/news/people/donald-trump-nigel-farage-photo-arron-banks-raheem-kassam-andy-wigmore-garry-gunster-a7416836.html.

Ouellette, Laurie, and Sarah Banet-Weiser. 2018. "Special Issue: Media and the Extreme Right: Editor's Introduction." *Communication, Culture and Critique* 11, no. 1: 1–6.

Phillips, Whitney. 2016. *This Is Why We Can't Have Nice Things: Mapping the Relationship between Online Trolling and Mainstream Culture*. Cambridge, MA: MIT Press.

Piketty, Thomas. 2014. *Capital in the Twenty-First Century*. Cambridge, MA: Belknap.

Reuters. 2015. "American Referendum Veteran Hired to Persuade Britons to Leave EU." *Guardian*, October 9. www.theguardian.com/politics/2015/oct/09/american-hired-brexit-eu-referendum-gerry-gunster.

Robataille, Stacia (@staciaRR). 2017. "#ThisIsOur President." Twitter, December 11, 6:25 p.m. twitter.com/staciarr/status/940407146583179264.

Rose, Gillian. 2012. *Visual Methodologies*. 3rd ed. London: Sage.

Sassen, Saskia. 2015. *Losing Control? Sovereignty in the Age of Globalization*. New York: Columbia University Press.

Savage, Mike, and Karel Williams. 2008. "Elites: Remembered in Capitalism and Forgotten in Social Sciences." *Sociological Review* 56, no. 1: 1–24.

Sayer, Andrew. 2016. *Why We Can't Afford the Rich*. Bristol, UK: Policy.

Senft, Terri. 2008. *Camgirls: Celebrity and Community in the Age of Social Media*. Bern: Peter Lang.

Trump, Donald J., with Tony Schwartz. 1987. *The Art of the Deal*. New York: Random House.

Wagstaff, Keith. 2016. "Men of the People Nigel Farage and Donald Trump Pose in Golden Elevator." *Mashable*, November 13. mashable.com/2016/11/13/donald-trump-and-nigel-farage-golden-elevator/.

Walker, Peter. 2016. "Donald Trump on Steroids: The Controversial Rise of Farage Favourite and Breitbart UK Editor Raheem Kassam." *Independent*, December 2. www.independent.co.uk/news/uk/politics/raheem-kassam-breitbart-editor-profile-who-is-he-farage-favourite-donald-trump-on-steroids-a7445821.html.

Weaver, Matthew, and Jim Waterson. 2018. "Leave.EU Fined £70,000 over Breaches of Electoral Law." *Guardian*, May 11. www.theguardian.com/politics/2018/may/11/leaveeu-fined-70k-breaches-of-electoral-law-eu-referendum.

Younge, Gary. 2018. "Middletown, America." Podcast. New Economics Foundation, March 5. neweconomics.org/2018/03/weekly-economics-podcast-middletown-america-gary-younge.

Jo Littler is a reader in the Department of Sociology at City, University of London. She is part of the editorial collective of *Soundings: A Journal of Politics and Culture*, an editor of the *European Journal of Cultural Studies*, and author of *Against Meritocracy: Culture, Power, and Myths of Mobility* (2018).

MEDIA REPRESENTATIONS of the NOUVEAUX RICHES and the CULTURAL CONSTITUTION of the GLOBAL MIDDLE CLASS

Jennifer Smith Maguire

Abstract The article offers a distinctive account of how the nouveaux riches serve as an anchor for a range of upper-middle-class ambivalences and anxieties associated with transformations of capitalism and shifting global hierarchies. Reflecting the long-term association of middle-class symbolic boundaries with notions of refinement and respectability, it examines how the discourse of civility shapes how the nouveaux riches are represented to the upper middle class, identifying a number of recurrent media frames and narrative tropes related to vulgarity, civility, and order. The author argues that these representations play a central role in the reproduction of the Western professional middle class, and in the cultural constitution of a *global* middle class—professional, affluent, urban, and affiliated by an aesthetic regime of civility that transcends national borders. The findings underline the significance of representations of the new super-rich as devices through which the media accomplish the global circulation of an upper-middle-class repertoire of cultural capital, which is used both to police shifting class boundaries and to establish a legitimate preserve for univorous snobbishness.

Keywords civility, media, middle class, nouveaux riches, vulgarity

In dialogue with the special issue theme, this article examines the question—and, in turn, the response—that the nouveau super-rich pose for the identity of the professional

Cultural Politics, Volume 15, Issue 1, © 2019 Duke University Press
DOI: 10.1215/17432197-7289472

middle class. As affluent and cosmopolitan as they may be, the professional class remains located as a middle class between—and as—labor and ownership, with their reproduction far from assured, as their children must compete through education and occupation to maintain their middle-class status. These structural conditions of existence are set against changing macro conditions of capitalism, which include not only new cadres of the super-rich but also new middle classes of emerging economies with whom the Western professional classes (and their children) now compete. Such large-scale processes have disrupted the context within which the upper middle classes experience their class position, unsettled their positionality vis-à-vis other groups, and laid the foundations for the emergence of a "global middle class" (Andreotti, Le Galès, and Moreno-Fuentes 2014; Koo 2016): professional, affluent, urban, and—as I argue in this article—affiliated through a discursive regime of civility that is deployed in relation to the nouveaux riches.

Specifically, the article presents an analysis of how the nouveaux riches are represented in media aimed at the Western professional middle class (US and UK quality/broadsheet newspapers). Reflecting the long-term association of middle-class symbolic boundaries with notions of refinement and respectability (Freeman 2012; Liechty 2012), I explore how a discourse of civility shapes how the new rich are framed. Far from merely representing status anxiety and/or an alibi for the "modest" wealth of the professional middle class (cf. Jaworksi and Thurlow 2017), the article offers a distinctive account of the role of representations of the nouveaux riches as anchors for a range of upper-middle-class ambivalences and anxieties associated with transformations

of capitalism and shifting global hierarchies. I argue that representations of the nouveaux riches play a central role in the cultural constitution of the global middle class, serving as significant devices through which the media accomplish the global circulation of an upper-middle-class repertoire of cultural capital, which is used both to police shifting class boundaries and to establish a legitimate preserve for univorous snobbishness (Peterson 2005), if not also crude racism and colonial condescension. In so doing, I identify global commonalities within upper-middle-class discourse, addressing the lack of research thus far on the character and ideological dispositions of the global middle class, and its symbolic boundaries and strategies of class reproduction (Koo 2016: 444).

Class and Civility

The middle class is a relational concept, defined as a social process of interrelations between groups structurally differentiated "crucially, but not exclusively" by productive relations (Thompson 1978: 149). My particular focus is the interrelationship and symbolic boundaries between the "established" upper middle class (Western, professional, affluent) and the nouveaux riches who—despite their superior economic power—are nevertheless positioned as "outsiders" in the global world order (Elias [1939] 2012). Since the 1970s, a range of developments have been reshaping the constitution of these groups, and the "established/outsider relations" (Elias and Scotson [1965] 1994) between them. Developments within finance, banking, high-tech industries, and celebrity culture—and more generally the financialization of capitalism—have generated new tiers of wealth, exacerbating the income and education gaps between the wealthiest and the rest (e.g., Fischer and Mattson

2009; Kendall 2011; Lapavitsas 2013). Furthermore, the occupational prospects, rewards, and autonomy of the Western "professional-managerial class" have been sharply reconfigured through neoliberalism and globalization (Ehrenreich and Ehrenreich 1979, 2013): the expanded demand for services has pulled their occupations into increasingly managerial and bureaucratic structures, and the intensifying offshoring of professional services has placed them in competition with emerging economies' middle classes. The elite "global middle class" (Andreotti, Le Galès, and Moreno-Fuentes 2014; Koo 2016) thus faces the challenge of making sense of itself in relation not only to its local class factions but also, variously, to its global peers, as well as the global-scale middle classes (Heiman, Liechty, and Freeman 2012), and the stratospheric rise of the nouveau super-rich.

Besides its relationality, middle classness is understood to "eventuate" through "regularities of response" in the ways that people behave (Thompson 1978: 147). A key characteristic of the middle classes' regularities of response—evidenced across time and space—has been respectability and refinement, typically played out through the sphere of consumption (e.g., Archer and Blau 1993; Mosse 1985; Schielke 2012; Skeggs 1997; Wilson 1973). On the one hand, middle-class respectability is constructed in opposition to the (profligate, morally suspect) consumption habits of the working and upper classes (e.g., Freeman 2012; Liechty 2012). On the other, middle-brow, middle-class concerns with respectability are linked to excessive status-oriented consumption (e.g., Frank 2007; Koo 2016; Schor 1999; Veblen [1899] 1959). As Pierre Bourdieu (1984: 249) summarizes: "Where the petit bourgeois or nouveau riche 'overdoes it,'

betraying his own insecurity, bourgeois discretion signals its presence by a sort of ostentatious discretion, sobriety and understatement, a refusal of everything which is 'showy,' 'flashy' and pretentious, and which devalues itself by the very intention of distinction." Respectability and refinement thus underpin divisions within the middle classes, and between those "below" and "above" them.

Refinement and respectability are nested within the much larger, longer-term legitimacy framework of the discourse of civility. Codes of conduct (associated with self-restraint, foresight, deferred gratification, elaborated manners, and so forth) have developed from the Middle Ages under the banner of "civility," first within the upper classes and then spreading from the nineteenth century onward "across the rising lower classes of Western society and over the various classes in the colonies" (Elias [1939] 2012: 470). Over time, established groups (those with greater capacity to claim group status and ascribe inferior positions to "outsiders") have repeatedly colonized outsiders via these codes of conduct and notions of civility (imposed by the established and copied by the outsiders), and then, finding their position of dominance subject to unwanted challenges, have sought to consolidate barriers between groups through more elaborated codes of conduct.

These patterns of assimilation and differentiation—repeated across the long history of modernity—attest to the importance of a strict code of manners: "It is an instrument of prestige, but it is also—in a certain phase—an instrument of power. It is not a little characteristic of the structure of Western society that the watchword of its colonising movement is 'civilisation'" (Elias [1939] 2012: 474). The concern in this article is with how that

Jennifer Smith Maguire

discourse of civility continues in the present day to shape the symbolic boundaries around the upper middle class and—more generally—constitutes an aesthetic regime through which a *global* middle class constructs its sense of self.

Media Representations of the Nouveaux Riches

Class reproduction hinges not only on modes of economic organization and productive relations but also on the classed institutions that reproduce the logics, dispositions, and peculiar combinations of cultural and social capital that underpin class subjectivities (Bourdieu 1984; Heiman, Liechty, and Freeman 2012; Savage et al. 2015; Thompson 1978). Media representations are significant mechanisms of class reproduction, implicated in the codification and circulation of middle-class norms, values, and lifestyles (e.g., Bourdieu and Passeron 1977; Kendall 2011; Jaworksi and Thurlow 2017; Wood and Skeggs 2011). The article thus draws on an analysis of how the nouveaux riches are represented in media aimed at the professional middle class.

The media sample consisted of items (n = 157) featuring the phrases *nouveau riche* or *new rich* from the following UK, US, and international quality/broadsheet newspapers: the *Daily Telegraph*, *Times* (London), *Independent*, *New York Times*, *Financial Times*, Associated Press, and *China Daily*.[1] These titles are primarily focused on the middle class, as suggested by readership statistics.[2] Middle class (ABC1, higher, intermediate, and junior professional/managerial/administrative) readers make up 77 percent of the 2017 print and online audience for the *Independent*, 79 percent for *Daily Telegraph*, and 84 percent for *Times*. Moreover—as per the article's focus—the titles attract a

predominantly professional middle-class readership. Higher and intermediate professional/managerial/administrative (AB) readers make up 56 percent and 63 percent, respectively, of the *Daily Telegraph* and *Times* (print) audiences; similarly, *New York Times* readers' median household income is US$189,000, and *Financial Times* readers (18 percent of whom are millionaires) have a mean annual income of US$270,000.

A thematic analysis (Fereday and Muir-Cochrane 2006) began with descriptive, deductive coding of each media item as to who was being discussed as a member of the nouveaux riches, and what they were doing. This coding provided an overview, not to the contemporary new rich themselves (whose lived experiences and attitudes cannot be deduced from these representations), but to the cultural imaginary of the contemporary nouveaux riches as it is articulated by and for the professional middle classes.

First: who are the nouveaux riches? There was one dominant country of origin in the media sample, 33 percent of which focused exclusively or primarily on the Chinese new rich.[3] (The next most prominent group, the Russian new rich, were the focus of only 5 percent of the sample.) The Chinese nouveaux riches also appeared frequently within articles on the new rich from multiple countries, as in the following account of Paris Fashion Week:

On the front row at one show: three Chinese women in their twenties, dressed to the nines, with matching nose jobs, jotting down their orders on their phones, only slightly impeded by the diamond gobstoppers on their fingers. On a second front row: an Arab woman in a headscarf watches the princess dresses from behind her invite. Leaving a third show: a woman bitching in Russian-accented English, to a man who

CULTURAL POLITICS · 15:1 March 2019

32

may or may not be her husband, about another nameless woman: "She can't even afford ready-to-wear so why is she at couture?" In the loos at the Plaza Athénée hotel's restaurant, a favourite with the couture set: a young Indian woman shakes her wrists, each freighted with a giant jewel-encrusted cuff that wouldn't look out of place in the Tower of London. "From my mother-in-law," she says to her friend, sounding bored. (Murphy 2016a)[4]

While frequently included, China was not always featured in such lists. Other examples included "Russian oligarchs, Middle Eastern royalty and the families of African dictators" (Lichfield 2014) and "the new rich from places like the Middle East, Russia, Brazil and Azerbaijan" (Vogel 2012).

These lists are not disconnected from the actual distribution of ultra high net worth (UHNW) individuals, as mapped by a proliferation of "rich lists." However, the relative mismatch between distribution of wealth and representations is notable: 13 percent of global billionaires in 2016 were from China and Hong Kong (more generally: 25 percent from Asia), whereas 33 percent of the media sample focused on China (and 51 percent on Asia); the largest real concentration of the UHNW is in the United States and Western Europe (41 percent), whereas these countries of origin featured in only 14 percent of the representations.[5] The analysis suggests that the representations are less about the nouveaux riches per se than the preoccupations of those whose place in the established global order is challenged; they chart not the uneven global distribution of wealth but the uneven distribution of sources of global middle-class readers' anxieties about their place in the world.

Second: what are they doing? The vast majority of media items included reference to specific objects and practices of consumption. Most frequently represented were the expected hallmarks of affluent discerning lifestyles: 23 percent of the sample mentioned art, music, wine, and food. Also frequently mentioned were transport (prestige cars, jets, yachts)— 15 percent of the sample; personal services (e.g., nannies, butlers, bespoke personal financial and wealth management services)—12 percent; residential properties (as investments and aesthetic statements)—10 percent; elite locations and events—8 percent. Other notable accoutrements included watches, well-toned bodies, philanthropic activities, prestige pets, and well-spoken English as a second language. Such categories of consumption, divorced from their representational context, might suggest that the nouveaux riches know what they are doing in deploying the expected positional signifiers of wealth and power (e.g., Budd 2016; Spence 2016; Wealth-X 2017b). However, nouveau riche consumption was typically framed not as a legitimate, insider's pursuit or a sincere appreciation of legitimate culture but as a crass display of wealth. As in the report on Paris Fashion week quoted above (Murphy 2016a), media representations seem to be less about illustrating the global diaspora of the new rich (China, the Middle East, Russia, India meeting on the front row, no less) than about evidencing novice knowledge of what to buy and where to be seen, but not how to behave. That is, the objects and practices of nouveau riche consumption were framed in ways that converted them into positional signifiers of outsider status—as the remainder of the findings will explore.

Framing the Nouveaux Riches

Building on these insights, a theoretically informed analysis examined the dominant frames for the nouveaux riches.

Frames—in the form of durable category labels, narrative structures, repertoires of expression—organize experiences and perceptions, selectively prioritizing information such that some understandings, behaviors, and judgments come to seem right and taken for granted (e.g., Goffman 1974; Humphreys and Latour 2013). In light of the long-term association of the middle class with respectability and refinement, I examined how these themes reverberated in the representations in relation to two frames:

- Vulgarity (lacking decorum, refinement, self-control and otherwise morally or aesthetically illegitimate vis-à-vis conventions of the Western bourgeois cultural canon)
- Civility (demonstrating refinement, restraint, foresight, and otherwise discernment and performances in line with the established cultural canon)

Inductive coding within those frames was linked to conceptualizing relationships between vulgarity and civility; this resulted in a third, emergent frame:

- Order (making sense of relative group positions, interrelations, and transitions between vulgarity and civility)

These three frames and their supporting exemplar stories are detailed below.

Vulgarity

Given the predominantly pejorative use of the term *nouveau riche* in popular discourse, "vulgarity" was unsurprisingly the dominant frame. Coding found evidence of the vulgarity frame in 75 percent of the sample. This reflected the broadest sense of lacking the attributes of civilized conduct and discerning consumption,

which variously took the form of populist consumption (e.g., buying something just because it was a high-status brand), functional consumption (e.g., taking part in an activity to achieve the instrumental end of showing off), failed discerning consumption (e.g., inappropriate behavior in the context of established elite culture), and other forms of coarse or illicit behavior (cf. Smith Maguire and Lim 2015).

In 39 percent of the sample, ascriptions of vulgarity were evident via language that specifically conveyed a lack of self-control or propriety. The new rich (in the following examples, Chinese) were described as "hungrily acquisitive . . . ambitious and rapacious" (Anderlini 2015b) and "unscrupulous" (*China Daily* 2014), with "voracious appetites" (Shotter 2013), "garish and excessive" (Qin 2013) and "extravagant" (*China Daily* 2015a) tastes, and "gaudy and ludicrous" cities (Davies 2013). The new rich of North Korea were described as "indulging" (Parry 2015), the Americans as "missing . . . gentility" (Robinson 2015) and "adolescent" in their interests (Mount 2013b); meanwhile, the Iranians "show off" and "crave attention" (Erdbrink 2015). Indeed, showing off was a hallmark of representations of the new rich, invoked through various references: "golden iPhones [with] a bejewelled microphone" in Nigeria (Tompson 2014); walls decorated with "wings of thousands of exotic butterflies" in Brazil (Cuadros 2016a); and for the Chinese new rich, wildlife hunting served as a "naked display of wealth" (Zhu 2014), along with Steinway pianos "outfitted with diamonds and wood from Africa and India" (Hernández 2016) and Rolls-Royce saloons personalized with "gold, glitter and horse badges [to celebrate the Year of the Horse] . . . or 400 diamonds encrusted in the car" (Pagano 2014).

Similarly, engagement with established cultural fields was represented as functional and lacking in an appropriately discerning orientation: wine buyers who "don't really give a damn about what's inside the bottle" were characterized as "splashing out and speculating" (Samuel 2012); art buyers were drawn to "obvious images by blue chip artists" (Vogel 2012) or to achieving an instrumental aim to "telegraph their wealth and taste" (Vogel 2013a). In all of these ways, the new economic capital of the nouveaux riches was framed as illegitimate by virtue of how it was (mis)translated into cultural practices.

Lack of propriety also took the form of corruption. On the one hand, eleven items referenced corruption within business practices (e.g., tax evasion, infringement on others' intellectual property, bribes, nepotism, and inside connections to secure deals). For example, the Chinese new rich were characterized by their "lack of integrity in business" (*China Daily* 2014), Iraqi new rich secured "lucrative government contracts through connections and corruption" (Hendawi 2014), while Russia was described as "in the grip of a kleptocracy" (Marsh 2012). On the other hand, nine items explicitly framed membership of the new rich as morally corrosive in itself, as evidenced through car crashes, out-of-control youth, and other destructive side effects of nouveau riche lifestyles in, for example, Iran (Erdbrink 2015), Brazil (Cuadros 2016b), and China (*China Daily* 2015b). The implied associations between vulgarity, corruption, and new wealth were further reinforced through reference to Chinese President Xi Jinping's anticorruption campaign (launched in 2012), both in the media sample and far more widely in reports on the luxury goods sector, which has been significantly impacted by the campaign. Thus the new riches were

framed as ill-gotten gains, and not to be necessarily envied by the reader: what Diana Kendall (2011: 55) refers to as "sour-grapes" and "bad-apple" framings of the wealthy.

The dominant narrative trope consisted of stories of nouveau riche "vulgarians," spoiled by their new money and despoiling the established cultural fields into which they stumble. The following description of elite art auctions in China was one example:

> The culture of bidding is still novel, newly wealthy buyers are inexperienced, and the auction houses themselves are figuring things out as they go along. . . . At auctions here, despite the presence of well-trained, white-gloved attendants, casually dressed buyers munch on snacks from paper bags and chat on cellphones, creating a low-level din throughout the bidding. Purchasers of expensive paintings have been known to roll up their canvas, tuck it under an arm and stroll out into the night air. (Bowley and Barboza 2013)

Contrasting this behavior with their counterparts in the West (where auctions are "discreet, air-kissing affairs" and buyers are "veteran, elegantly dressed collectors who know one another" and conduct their bids with subtle gestures and hushed tones), the account categorized nouveau riche performances and appearances—and the nouveaux riches themselves—as illegitimate.

Similarly, an item on Royal Ascot recounted the established class's dismay at various changes they saw as debasing the event, such as the inability of the strict clothing rules to veil (if not curtail) the current popularity of tattoos, or the decision to sell places in the Royal Enclosure: "Pander any further to populism, or so the aficionados cry, and you threaten to let every vulgarian this side of Reading in. This is meant to be a week about selectiveness, about exclusivity, not about opening the floodgates to the nouveaux riches" (Brown 2013). While the journalist's tongue was at least partially in his cheek, the choice of *floodgates* is telling, speaking to the perceived lack of order that erupts around the new rich. In this cultural imaginary, the nouveaux riches are not only individually out of control but are part of a process run amok that threatens to overwhelm and wipe out the established upper-middle-class group. This discourse is reminiscent of late nineteenth- and early twentieth-century anxieties about public order (in Britain, related especially to class; in the United States, to ethnicity and immigration), directed at the "horny handed," "the great unwashed," and the fecundity of foreigners (e.g., Ewen and Ewen 2006; Pearson 1983). Reference was made to the "swell" or "swelling" ranks of nouveaux riches (Hernández 2016; Xu 2016; Scheiber and Cohen 2015; Liu 2016; Xie 2014a) and to markets being "flooded" with nouveau riche money and demands (Anderlini 2015b; Hook and Hornby 2017). Other references were to the number of billionaires "made" per week, both suggesting the flood of new money and denuding the newly rich actor of her or his agency, perseverance, or prudence and instead attributing credit to the (out-of-control) system of value creation. Financialized capitalism and its multiplier effect for the ill-gotten gains from illegitimate means (e.g., bribes, nepotism) and nonlegitimate fields (e.g., construction and tetra paks: Marsh 2012; Mount 2013a) was thus positioned as a threat to the established upper-middle-class order, undermining hard work as the legitimate discursive bedrock of wealth (Sherman 2017) and, more insidiously, facilitating a rising tide of newcomers.

Civility

Less prevalent than the vulgarity frame, the civility frame was evident in 27 percent of the sample. Such representations positioned nouveau riche tastes and practices as legitimate or becoming legitimate when they closely aligned with the established repertoire of bourgeois "good taste." For example, Seoul's Gangnam District was described as "elegant" and the locals' style as "sophisticated" (Shim 2013), the Chinese new rich as "increasingly worldly and sophisticated" (Anderlini 2015a), and the new rich generally as moving "away from show for its own sake towards knowledge, appreciation, craft and heritage—something with a story" (Jones 2015), with the new "keywords" of the global "One Percent" being "unostentatious, calm and discreet" (Trebay 2016).

Civility was associated with self-restraint and understatement: a shift from bling to bespoke, from objects to experiences. Wealthy Chinese consumers, for example, were noted for increasingly valuing "experiences rather than expensive products . . . [and] specifications and value rather than mere status symbols" (Bland 2016). Craftsmanship, heritage, bespoke construction, elegance, and subtlety were presented not only as qualities of interest to a growing number of nouveau riche consumers, but also as the readers' taken-for-granted criteria for legitimate, discerning consumption. The legitimation of nouveau riche economic capital was thus restricted to its transformation into the established group's forms of civilized conduct and cultural capital.

The central narrative trope consisted of stories of the "new aesthetes" who have seized the opportunities afforded by their wealth to emulate the aesthetic habitus of the professional middle class. This was typically carried out within established cultural fields such as art collecting. For instance, an American billionaire (whose new wealth derived from the science and technology sector) was credited as being a "serious" and "thorough" art collector (Vogel 2013b): these benedictions were delivered by the chief executive of the J. Paul Getty Trust (bearing the mantle of old money), and by a respected Chelsea art dealer (wielding the imprimatur of the established group by virtue of having "worked with many of today's biggest collectors"). In another example, a "former taxi driver turned billionaire" and his wife are among China's small group of major art collectors; their collecting is similarly legitimated by the president of Christie's China (the established auction house), who is quoted (Qin 2015) as describing the couple as the "'best example' of this generation of Chinese art collectors. 'They started with collecting what they know, Chinese art, then broadened to Asian art, and are now embracing Western art.'" Similarly, approving note was taken of those in Brazil who align with "an older tradition of wealth" (Cuadros 2016a) and of the "superrich from China and other emerging markets" who are "joining their *fellow elites* at events in Europe and the United States" (Frank 2015; emphasis added). Ascriptions of civility and legitimacy were thus dispensed in terms of acceptance of the new rich by the established elite and professional middle class.

Thorough absorption into the codes of civility extended from the obvious fields such as art and fashion to the quotidian matters of dress and appearance. For example, a young Chinese tech entrepreneur whose "rectangular black glasses, slim build, and red sweater seem inspired by the hipsters of Silicon Valley" was positioned as an exemplar of the "new

entrepreneurial class amassing great wealth at a younger age. . . . These risk-takers are sophisticated, often Western-educated, and comfortable working with foreign banks at home and dabbling in investments abroad" (Xu 2016). The new aesthetes thus become indistinguishable from the established group. Rather than being framed as a further "swelling" of the ranks of the new rich (or as an anxiety about the new rich using appearances to trick their way into acceptance, as was the discourse in the nineteenth century in relation to cosmetics; Peiss 1998), this transformation (of "them" into "us") was framed as a positive bolstering of the established group.

Despite the "success stories," the extension of legitimacy to the nouveaux riches was dampened by echoes of colonial snobbishness (e.g., as per the president of Christie's China, whose comments imply Western art is the apogee of a global hierarchy of cultural capital). Such representations suggest how tightly bound the discourse of civility is to notions of "the West," which have been constructed through an othering of "the rest" over the very long-term history of colonial and global expansion from the fifteenth century onward (Hall 1996). Similarly, media accounts of the new aesthetes were accompanied by parallel, delegitimizing associations. For example, a report on the new rich in Vietnam approvingly noted their increasing emphasis on hand-crafted, distinctive goods with provenance and their desire "to demonstrate their knowledge" (Cohen 2014). However, this "progress" was undercut by a story of a vulgarian: "A successful Vietnamese businessman confided to me that when he receives a gift of a bottle of Johnnie Walker Black Label (surely one of the world's great blended whiskies) he sends it back because it is insultingly ordinary." A shift from bling to subtlety was likewise framed as vulgar for the Chinese new rich: instead of showing off their wealth, they now "want to show their good taste, their personal choice" (Lin 2015). Be it through an instrumental orientation to taste or their hyper compliance with (and thus lack of aesthetic distance from) established aesthetic norms, such representations framed the nouveaux riches as delegitimizing themselves (thereby preserving the liberal values of the professional middle class, who are positioned as mere witnesses rather than agents of the stigmatization of others).

Order

The vulgarity and civility frames offered professional middle-class readers a sense of order for the turmoil of shifting concentrations of influence and capital, placing various new rich groups into a legible framework of relative positions: the illegitimate parvenus whose economic power may dwarf the readers' but who are nonetheless vulgar in their tastes; and the legitimate apprentice connoisseurs whose dispositions bolster the established group by reaffirming the currency of their cultural capital and rituals. At the same time, the tales of legitimate aesthetic discernment and consumption within the new rich—exemplified by the new aesthetes—make clear that nouveau riche membership is neither static nor immutable. For example, an item on China notes that the "Chinese nouveaux riches—until recently renowned for their awkward manners—already qualify as 'old money'; they're now comfortable in French restaurants, fluent in English and expert in vintage Chiantis" (Perrottet 2016). Such a transition has occurred in a relatively short period of time; as one report suggests,

"What would take 20 years in the West happens here in two to five years" (Armstrong 2012). This rate and scale of change inevitably creates tensions for those who find their place in the global hierarchy of power and esteem to have been diluted if not leap-frogged. As such, the media discourse of the nouveaux riches also served an ordering function, with regard to how the professional middle-class readers were positioned within the changing global order and were encouraged to understand the dynamics of that new order. The seeming happenstance or injustice of movement (e.g., the "sudden" riches of some outsiders) was thus subject to ordering and order-imposing frames, which attempted to bring sense and stability to a ground that was simultaneously depicted as shifting beneath the readers' feet.

The dominant narrative tropes were cosmologies: stories that placed the universe (in this case, the earthly distribution of economic and cultural capital) in an ordered framework governed by general principles. Cosmologies were manifest in a number of ways, including, first, various lists, lexicons, and maps of the world's elite. These have multiplied since the 1970s as part of the discursive construction of the rich and super-rich (Koh, Wissink, and Forrest 2016) and are often cited for corroboration and context in the media reports. A vocabulary of "the other" categorized the new rich into a legible taxonomy: for example, Chinese *tuhao*, *fu'erdai*, and *bao fa hu* (new rich, second generation, and rags-to-riches households, respectively); Iranian *aghazadeh*; Brazillionaires and *novos ricos*; Russian oligarchs; North Korea *donju*; Middle East plutocrats; and various other geographically situated clusters of tycoons, nabobs, magnates, and moneybags (e.g., Garst 2014; Hook and Hornby 2017; Vandervelde 2016; Erdbrink

2013; Cuadros 2016a, 2016b; Lichfield 2014; Fifield 2016; Vogel 2012). Internally stratified, globally dispersed groups of economic elites with varied repertoires of cultural competences and dispositions were thereby essentialized for readers.

Second, quasi-ethnographic travelogues provided the intended reader with a touristic overview of social hierarchies from various locales and times. For example, the life stages of the new rich consumer were neatly summarized in a Shanghai travelogue:

First they go for the shiny, brash stuff. Then they progress to the more discreet emblems of consumption. Finally they graduate to bespoke. The Chinese have achieved maturity at break-neck speed. That doesn't mean there aren't molls with surgically rounded eyes and pumped-up lips wearing Cavalli—but not nearly as many as there were in Russia in the early oligarch years. (Armstrong 2012)

Stories of enhanced female companions in low-cut dresses, butterfly wing–decorated walls, diamond encrusted iPhones, and Maseratis crashed by spoiled children of the elite all provide grist for the vulgarization mill. However, such stories also fuel—sometimes quite explicitly—the anxiety of the reader, affirming that their place in the world is no longer to be taken for granted. For example, an Indonesian journalist quips at an elite event in China: "Europe is finished. . . . Shanghai's the city of the 21st century" (Armstrong 2012); and nouveau riche Americans declare that "no one cares" about old money, which is "living on fumes" (Robinson 2015). Meanwhile, an esteemed British financial journalist opines that the British "are making the luxury items that most of us can't afford" (McRae 2013) and wonders, "How will European attitudes to wealth

shift when we realise that we are, in relative terms at least, not as rich as we used to be?" (McRae 2014). These accounts, from a bird's-eye view, revealed overlapping, multiscalar, multilocal established/outsider relations between old money, the new rich, and the professional middle classes (and occasionally the lower-middle and working classes), within and across Western and emerging economies. Global, complex changes are thus reduced to a simplified story of change and the status quo (the outsiders become the established; *plus ça change*) within which readers may locate themselves (albeit with some trepidation).

Third, discrete devices imposed a sense of order on movements within cosmologies: progress between positions over time was attributed to particular strategies and was thereby rationalized, and—depending on the framing—rendered illegitimate or legitimate. On the one hand, some movements were delegitimized, and the acquisition devices and strategies framed as at least partially vulgar. In such cases, the pursuit of cultural capital was often framed as an instrumental (vulgar) pursuit of status, be that on the part of the state—for example, Chinese policy to support regional development through art, music, yachting (e.g., Hernández 2016; Xie 2014b)—or individuals. Individual acquisition strategies were often oriented to removing the established group's habitus and language advantages, such as through private European or American education (e.g., Bland 2016; C. Li 2016; Yen 2013; Malvern 2015), hiring Filipino nannies who "often teach the children better English" (Cheung 2016), enrolling in finishing schools to learn such skills as "Western table manners, floral arrangement, table conversation, dress codes" (*China Daily* 2016), or, for those aspiring to middle-class status within the outsider group, enrolling in butler school to learn a "whole range of Western etiquette and protocols, from personal grooming to laying tables and pouring wine" (Y. Li 2016). For the seriously wealthy, acquisition strategies were oriented to joining, if not displacing, the established elite. For example, a Chinese art collector is quoted in regard to his rationale for paying a record-setting price at auction ($170.4 million with fees): "Every museum dreams of having a Modigliani nude. . . . Now, a Chinese museum has a globally recognized masterpiece . . . I feel very proud about that. . . . The message to the West is clear: We have bought their buildings, we have bought their companies, and now we are going to buy their art" (Qin 2015). The collector's motivation is framed as not only illegitimate—instrumental position seeking rather than sincere appreciation—but also menacing, suggesting the long-term and highly contentious cultural dynamics associated with decentering the West (Hall 1996).

On the other hand, movements were more likely to be framed as legitimate when attributable to the pedagogical interventions deployed by the established group to transfer their cultural capital and habitus to worthy outsiders (albeit arguably in pursuit of vulgar ends: the creation of new luxury goods consumers). Such "civilizing" interventions took the form of various immersive lifestyle lessons intended to serve as a transmission belt, pulling the new rich in to the established habitus of the elite and remaking them as the "branded gentry" (Vallance and Hopper 2013; Smith 2016). Examples from the sample include Louis Vuitton experts teaching Shanghai customers the refined art of packing (Armstrong 2012); London's Harrods and Selfridges finessing access

to fashion shows and horse races for their Chinese shoppers so that they can "discover the British lifestyle, dressing codes and etiquette" (Lin 2015); Rolls-Royce partnering with an eminent London tailor to create events that educate the young, British new rich in "the story of bespoke" (Murphy 2016b); the contemporary Istanbul art fair aiming to educate the Turkish new rich "in the culture of collecting art" (Adam 2012); private banks offering the nouveaux riches of Asia, Middle East, Eastern Europe, and Latin America such perks as wine tastings with royalty, private seminars with prestigious thinkers, yachting classes, golf trips, and "mock art auctions to teach newly rich how to bid on expensive paintings" (Weinland and Noonan 2016).

Within these stories of legitimate mobility, the place of the global middle class was often represented by a cast of "functional democratizers" (Smith Maguire 2017): Pygmalion heroes whose status rested in part on their ability to straddle worlds and bridge groups. Such heroes included the Chinese "heir" to a musical instrument company, educated in the United States, who fine-tunes the Chinese mind-set about quality craftsmanship and Steinway pianos (Hernández 2016); the Dutch "veteran butler" and descendant of a "butlering family" who teaches the aspiring Chinese butlers how to embody and service cultural capital (Y. Li 2016); the editor of Chinese *Vogue*, "daughter of a Chinese diplomat, married to an Englishman," who holidays in Britain and "speaks English like a BBC pro" (Armstrong 2013); the Chinese-American couturier whose Shanghai flagship store in a 1920s heritage villa in the French Concession includes "a showroom, fitting salons, an art gallery, a library, a fashion lounge and a VIP suite" because she wants to offer "a sharing space for people who have the same tastes and ideas" (Sun 2016).

Mobilities within hierarchies of wealth and power were thus represented as legitimate or illegitimate via intersections between a range of ordering lexicons, stories, devices, and heroes, and vulgarity and civility frames. The cosmologies thus reproduce the currency of the established group's stocks of cultural capital as the legitimate basis of worthy entitlement (Fluck 2003; Sherman 2017). In turn, the professional middle class are offered an account that reassures them of their place—and competitive advantage—within new global hierarchies. Indeed, the very admission of movement within the cosmologies upholds established parables of meritocracy that underpin the legitimation of inequality (Littler 2018). These cosmological narratives thus impose a taxonomy of positions, simplify complex processes into a repeated, legible pattern of change, rationalize and (de)legitimate movement between positions, and reassure the global middle class that their status as bastions of respectability and civility remains largely unchallenged.

Discussion and Conclusion

In this article, I have been concerned with how the discourse of civility is implicated in the cultural constitution of the professional middle class, as effected through media representations of the nouveaux riches, and what that might suggest about the character of a global middle class. Underpinning the media representations are changing political, economic, and cultural currents—emerging markets and their middle classes, a new Gilded Age of financialized capitalism with the super-rich 0.1 percent (and especially 0.01 percent) pulling away from the rest. These conditions challenge the professional middle

classes' local identities and positions and create the conditions for a transnational upper middle class to articulate its identity through the watchword of civility.

From the analysis there emerged an essentializing framing of the nouveaux riches through country of origin and a constellation of consumption performances that (despite being oriented to the ostensibly correct objects) signaled outsider status. The analysis further revealed a range of dominant frames and narrative tropes through which the nouveaux riches were positioned as illegitimate or legitimate, in turn rendering the upper-middle-class readership legible to itself. On the one hand, undeserving vulgarians were stigmatized and positioned as emblematic of larger outsider groups (the new super-rich and new middle classes of emerging economies) against whom the professional middle class was juxtaposed. On the other, new aesthetes were legitimated insofar as they reproduced the currency of established cultural capital, thereby bolstering the class identity of the professional middle class.

Several limitations of this analysis bear mention, indicating work still to be done to complement these insights. In focusing on representations in isolation from their production and reception, I have assumed that recurrent patterns in media frames and tropes are constitutive—and thus indicative—of class identities. In taking journalists as proxies for the larger professional middle class, I have sidestepped differences within their ranks vis-à-vis their professional orientation to the nouveaux riches (e.g., art critics, fashion reporters, financial journalists) and bracketed off questions of the journalists' habitus, thus ignoring differences in their class identities, stocks of cultural capital, and so on. I have also had to overlook the

Jennifer Smith Maguire

role of occupational and genre conventions in shaping media representations. These shortcomings suggest the need for further explorations of the lived experience of professional middle-class identities. Furthermore, in focusing on patterns shared across the seven media titles, I have ignored the distinct historical and contemporary contexts that shape national class identities (especially British and American). Nevertheless, the commonalities identified—spanning readerships and globally disparate nouveau riche objects—suggest the outlines of a global middle-class identity, which demands further attention and cross-cultural investigation.

The intersections between ordering, vulgarity, and civility frames speak to the interlinked spasms of attraction and repulsion, colonization and differentiation (Elias [1939] 2012), that continue to shape the group identity and symbolic boundaries of the middle classes. Framing nouveau riche consumption as crass excess and vulgar spectacle, or as legitimate apprenticeship in the class habitus of the upper middle class, can thus be understood as a strategy by which the established—and threatened—professional middle class attempts to defend their group identity in an age in which the relative dominance of the West has been fundamentally challenged. Moreover, the findings suggest how the emergence and reproduction of local and global professional middle classes are deeply embedded within the long-held symbolic practices and narrative structures of civility. Civility operates as a global aesthetic regime that transcends national differences while allowing for local variations in how civility is performed: concerns with both manners and morals can be filtered through the lens of civility.

The cosmologies of civility that characterized the media representations

underpin a naturalization of stratification and inequality as part of that global middle-class mentality, without contravening middle-class democratic values. From ancient times, hierarchical cosmological metaphors—*scala naturae*—have reflected and shaped human thought about the categories of and relations between orders of being. Epitomized in the medieval "Great Chain of Being," these inventories of existence were often depicted as a multitiered tree, staircase, or ladder culminating in God (Lovejoy 1936; Guyer 2010). Despite intervening scientific and philosophical developments—from rationalism to progressivism, natural selection, evolution, and critical theorizations of class reproduction and inequality—Western peoples, including the intelligentsia, "maintain a deep allegiance" to these medieval metaphors (Pavelka McDonald 2002; see also Guyer 2010) that naturalize the dominance of particular groups over others (e.g., humans over animals, kings over commoners). The frames and cosmologies of civility that emerged from the media analysis may be more complex than the medieval *scala naturae*, but the principles remain the same: a place for each group and each group to its place, with the stratification of positions consecrated by a higher order of legitimacy (the bourgeois cultural canon replacing Divine Will).

Such deep-seated narrative structures and aesthetic regimes are crucial for the reproduction of inequality, as they tend to elide contradictions between explicitly rejecting ideas of the natural superiority of some over others, while simultaneously holding—and acting on—biases that uphold those same ideas about relative worth. This helps explain how the middle classes maintain implicit prowealth attitudes that grant greater leniency to those of higher socioeconomic status, while also espousing egalitarian attitudes and even negative stereotypes about the rich (Horwitz and Dovidio 2017). The nouveau riche figure plays a central part in the articulation of these cosmologies of civility, through which upper-middle-class anxieties about out-of-control capitalism are placed within a coherent framework of civilized stratification. In this way, the discourse of civility allows snobbishness to "go underground" (Savage et al. 2015): discussions of the nouveaux riches thus serve as a legitimate preserve for univorous (if not also colonialist) snobbishness within the wider culture of liberalism, meritocracy, and tolerance.

Acknowledgments

This article was made possible through research support from the University of Leicester's Research Institute for Cultural and Media Economies (CAMEo), and through a period of study leave granted by the University of Leicester College of Social Sciences, Arts and Humanities. My thanks in particular to Paula Serafini for assistance with the initial coding of the media sample, and Joseph Maguire and Angus Cameron for constructive suggestions on an earlier draft.

Notes

1. The search utilized the Nexis database, with the search terms *nouveau riche*, *nouveaux riches*, or *new rich* appearing anywhere in items from January 2012 to July 2017. A preliminary search of the *Daily Telegraph*, *Independent*, *Financial Times, New York Times*, and *Times* (London) revealed a preponderance of articles about the Chinese nouveaux riches; as such, *China Daily* and the Associated Press were added to ensure international readership, complementing the *Financial Times* readership, which is over two-thirds non-UK based (Beckett 2018). The search of the seven sources yielded a total of 508 hits; these were hand sorted to include only those items with explicit mention of the contemporary nouveaux riches (individuals and/or generic references to the new rich as a group). The final sample consisted of 157 media items.

2. Readership statistic sources, accessed in January 2018: National Readership Survey (NRS) October 2016–September 2017 readership data (www.nrs.co.uk); newsworks Fast Facts—Titles at a Glance (www.newsworks.org.uk); *New York Times* media kit (nytmediakit.com/newspaper); *Financial Times* media kit (www.fttoolkit.co.uk/d /audience/consumer.php). NRS audience categories relating to the middle class: higher (A), intermediate (B), and junior (C1) managerial, administrative, and professional occupations.

3. To guard against inflation, this count excluded the twenty-nine *China Daily* items, which all focused exclusively on Chinese new rich.

4. Page numbers are not available from Nexis searches.

5. Data on top thirty countries of the 2016 distribution of billionaires from Wealth-X (2017a). It is also interesting to note that the same Wealth-X report suggests the divisions of old/new within the UHNW: the wealth of only 13 percent of billionaires is attributable to inherited wealth, and self-made billionaires outnumber those who are a combination of self-made and inherited wealth by about 1.75 to 1.

References

Adam, Georgina. 2012. "Turkey's Stuffed Calendar." *New York Times*, December 1.

Anderlini, Jamil. 2015a. "Louis Vuitton Feels Mainland Pressure." *Financial Times*, November 17.

Anderlini, Jamil. 2015b. "Vintage Insights into China's Effect on the Business of Wine." *Financial Times*, November 12.

Andreotti, Alberta, Patrick Le Galès, and Francisco Javier Moreno-Fuentes. 2014. *Globalised Minds, Roots in the City: Urban Upper-Middle Classes in Europe.* Chichester, UK: Wiley.

Archer, Melanie, and Judith R. Blau. 1993. "Class Formation in Nineteenth-Century America: The Case of the Middle Class." *Annual Review of Sociology* 19: 17–41.

Armstrong, Lisa. 2013. "Chinese Whisper: Bling's Had Its Day." *Daily Telegraph*, November 15.

Armstrong, Lisa. 2012. "The New Orient Express." *Daily Telegraph*, July 25.

Beckett, Andy. 2018. "How to Spend It: The Shopping List for the One Percent." *Guardian*, July 19.

Bland, Ben. 2016. "Hong Kong Loses Its Status as the Great Mall Of China." *Financial Times*, September 12.

Bourdieu, Pierre. 1984. *Distinction: A Social Critique of the Judgement of Taste.* Cambridge, MA: Harvard University Press.

Bourdieu, Pierre, and Jean-Claude Passeron. 1977. *Reproduction in Education, Society, and Culture.* London: Sage.

Bowley, Graham, and David Barboza. 2013. "China's Art Market Powerhouse Complicates Reform Efforts." *New York Times*, December 16.

Brown, Oliver. 2013. "Royal Enclosure for £500? It Is Ascot, but Not as We Know It." *Daily Telegraph*, June 20.

Budd, Lucy. 2016. "Flights of Indulgence (Or How the Very Wealthy Fly): The Aeromobile Patterns and Practices of the Super-Rich." In *Handbook on Wealth and the Super-Rich*, edited by Iain Hay and Jonathan V. Beaverstock, 302–21. Cheltenham, UK: Edward Elgar.

Cheung, Gloria. 2016. "China's New Rich Fuel Black Market in Filipino Nannies." *Financial Times*, October 1.

China Daily. 2014. "Tuhao for Want of a Better Word." *China Daily*, September 1.

China Daily. 2015a. "An Equestrian Wedding." *China Daily*, March 9.

China Daily. 2015b. "Drivers of Beijing's 'Fast And Furious' Car Race Sentenced." *China Daily*, May 21.

China Daily. 2016. "Female Entrepreneur Teaches Etiquette to Wealthy Chinese." *China Daily*, August 25.

Cohen, Roger. 2014. "Status in the New Asia." *New York Times*, May 13.

Cuadros, Alex. 2016a. "Meet the Brazillionaires." *Independent*, June 1.

Cuadros, Alex. 2016b. "The Brazillionaire." *Times* (London), July 16.

Davies, Paul J. 2013. "Surge in Asian Millionaire Clients Provides Lucrative Opportunities." *Financial Times*, November 29.

Ehrenreich, Barbara, and John Ehrenreich. 1979. "The Professional-Managerial Class" In *Between Labor and Capital: The Professional-Managerial Class*, edited by Pat Walker, 5–45. Boston: South End.

Ehrenreich, Barbara, and John Ehrenreich. 2013. *Death of a Yuppie Dream: The Rise and Fall of the Professional-Managerial Class.* New York: Rose Luxemburg Stiftung.

Elias, Norbert. (1939) 2012. *On the Process of Civilisation.* Dublin: University College Dublin Press.

Elias, Norbert, and John L. Scotson. (1965) 1994. *The Established and the Outsiders: A Sociological Enquiry into Community Problems.* 2nd ed. London: Sage.

Erdbrink, Thomas. 2013. "Iran's Hard-Liners Keep Their Criticism of Nuclear Pact to Themselves." *New York Times*, December 2.

Erdbrink, Thomas. 2015. "Fatal Car Crash Unleashes Anger at Iran's Elites." *New York Times*, May 1.

Ewen, Stuart, and Elizabeth Ewen. 2006. *Typecasting: On the Arts and Sciences of Human Inequality.* New York: Seven Stories.

Fereday, Jennifer, and Eimear Muir-Cochrane. 2006. "Demonstrating Rigor Using Thematic Analysis: A Hybrid Approach of Inductive and Deductive Coding and Theme Development." *International Journal of Qualitative Methods* 5, no. 1: 1–11.

Fifield, Anna. 2016. "North Korea: Rich Kids of the People's Republic Savour Life in 'Pyonghattan.'" *Independent*, May 15.

Fischer, Claude S., and Greggor Mattson. 2009. "Is America Fragmenting?" *Annual Review of Sociology* 35: 435–55.

Fluck, Winfried. 2003. "What Is So Bad about Being Rich? The Representation of Wealth in American Culture." *Comparative American Studies* 1, no. 1: 53–79.

Frank, Robert. 2007. *Falling Behind: How Rising Inequality Harms the Middle Class.* Berkeley: University of California Press.

Frank, Robert. 2015. "For the New Superrich, Life Is Much More Than a Beach." *New York Times*, June 21.

Freeman, Carla. 2012. "Neoliberal Respectability: Entrepreneurial Marriage, Affective Labor, and a New Caribbean Middle Class" In *The Global Middle Classes: Theorizing through Ethnography*, edited by Rachel Heiman, Carla Freeman, and Mark Liechty, 85–115. Santa Fe, NM: School for Advanced Research Press.

Garst, William Daniel. 2014. "Why Tuhao Year-End Bonus Matters." *China Daily*, January 30.

Goffman, Erving. 1974. *Frame Analysis: An Essay on the Organization of Experience*. Boston: Northeastern University Press.

Guyer, Jane I. 2010. "The Eruption of Tradition? On Ordinality and Calculation." *Anthropological Theory* 10, nos. 1–2: 123–31.

Hall, Stuart. 1996. "The West and the Rest: Discourse and Power." In *Modernity: An Introduction to Modern Societies*, edited by Stuart Hall, David Held, Don Hubert, and Kenneth Thompson, 184–228. Oxford: Blackwell.

Heiman, Rachel, Mark Liechty, and Carla Freeman. 2012. "Introduction: Charting an Anthropology of the Middle Class." In *The Global Middle Classes: Theorizing through Ethnography*, edited by Rachel Heiman, Carla Freeman, and Mark Liechty, 3–29. Santa Fe, NM: School for Advanced Research Press.

Hendawi, Hamza. 2014. "Dark Days for Baghdad on Eve of Iraqi Elections." Associated Press, April 28.

Hernández, Javier C. 2016. "Grand Ambitions in China." *New York Times*, July 10.

Hook, Leslie, and Lucy Hornby. 2017. "Murder Case Highlights China-US Money Trail." *Financial Times*, May 19.

Horwitz, Suzanne R., and John F. Dovidio. 2017. "The Rich—Love Them or Hate Them? Divergent Implicit and Explicit Attitudes toward the Wealthy." *Group Processes and Intergroup Relations* 20, no. 1: 3–31.

Humphreys, Ashlee, and Kathryn A. Latour. 2013. "Framing the Game: Assessing the Impact of Cultural Representations on Consumer Perceptions of Legitimacy." *Journal of Consumer Research* 40, no. 4: 773–95.

Jaworksi, Adam, and Crispin Thurlow. 2017. "Mediatizing the 'Super-Rich': Normalizing Privilege." *Social Semiotics* 27, no. 3: 276–87.

Jones, Mark. 2015. "Trancoso, Brazil: What Does 'New Luxury' Mean?" *Independent*, January 9.

Kendall, Diana. 2011. *Framing Class: Media Representations of Wealth and Poverty in America*. 2nd ed. Lanham, MD: Rowman and Littlefield.

Koh, Sin Yee, Bart Wissink, and Ray Forrest. 2016. "Reconsidering the Super-Rich: Variations, Structural Conditions, and Urban Consequences." In *Handbook on Wealth and the Super-Rich*, edited by Iain Hay and Jonathan V. Beaverstock, 18–40. Cheltenham, UK: Edward Elgar.

Koo, Hagen. 2016. "The Global Middle Class: How Is It Made, What Does It Represent?" *Globalizations* 13, no. 4: 440–53.

Lapavitsas, Costas. 2013. "The Financialization of Capitalism: 'Profiting without Producing.'" *City* 17, no. 6: 792–805.

Li, Cao. 2016. "Q. and A.: Zhang Fan on Chinese 'Parachute Kids' in the U.S." *New York Times*, March 2.

Li, Yang. 2016. "The School That Serves Up Butlers." *China Daily*, February 1.

Lichfield, John. 2014. "What the Foch? Plan to Redevelop Paris's Richest Road into Park, Shopping Mall and Council Estate." *Independent*, January 22.

Liechty, Mark. 2012. "Middle-Class Déjà Vu: Conditions of Possibility, from Victorian England to Contemporary Kathmandu." In *The Global Middle Classes: Theorizing through Ethnography*, edited by Rachel Heiman, Carla Freeman, and Mark Liechty, 271–99. Santa Fe, NM: School for Advanced Research Press.

Lin, Jinghua. 2015. "Luxury Is in the Wallet of the Beholder." *China Daily*, October 31.

Littler, Jo. 2018. *Against Meritocracy: Culture, Power, and Myths of Mobility*. London: Routledge.

Liu, Weiling. 2016. "Big Brands in the Bag." *China Daily*, June 1.

Lovejoy, Arthur O. 1936. *The Great Chain of Being: A Study of the History of an Idea*. Cambridge, MA: Harvard University Press.

Malvern, Jack. 2015. "Suffering Sloane Rangers Driven into Exile." *Times* (London), February 19.

Marsh, Stefanie. 2012. "How Much Am I Worth?" *Times* (London), November 24.

McRae, Hamish. 2013. "The West's New Role: Supplier of Luxury We Can't Afford Ourselves." *Independent*, July 10.

McRae, Hamish. 2014. "There Is a New Economic Faultline Dividing the World." *Independent*, June 11.

Mosse, George. 1985. *Nationalism and Sexuality: Respectability and Abnormal Behavior in Modern Europe*. New York: Fertig.

Mount, Harry. 2013a. "Erasing the Past." *New York Times*, October 20.

Mount, Harry. 2013b. "These Days You'll Only Find a Gatsby in Films." *Independent*, May 19.

Murphy, Anna. 2016a. "Six Figures for a Dress? The Most Expensive Frocks in the World." *Times* (London), February 3.

Murphy, Anna. 2016b. "Who Are the New Rich and What Do They Want?" *Times* (London), October 1.

Pagano, Margareta. 2014. "Rolls-Royce Is on a Roll as the Super-Rich Get All Revved Up." *Independent*, January 9.

Parry, Richard Lloyd. 2015. "Capitalist Property Boom Hits North Korea." *Times* (London), April 18.

Pavelka McDonald, Mary S. 2002. "Change versus Improvement over Time and Our Place in Nature." *Current Anthropology* 43, no. S4: S37–S44.

Pearson, Geoffrey. 1983. *Hooligan: A History of Respectable Fears*. London: Macmillan.

Peiss, Kathy. 1998. *Hope in a Jar: The Making of American Beauty Culture*. New York: Henry Holt.

Perrottet, Tony. 2016. "Tourists Gone Wild." *New York Times*, December 11.

Peterson, Richard A. 2005. "Problems in Comparative Research: The Example of Omnivorousness." *Poetics* 33, nos. 5–6: 257–82.

Qin, Amy. 2013. "Yet Another Way to Mock China's New Rich." *New York Times*, October 15.

Qin, Amy. 2015. "Dreaming of an Even Bigger Canvas." *New York Times*, November 18.

Robinson, Phil. 2015. "There Are New Rules for the Wealthy Now." *Times* (London), July 20.

Samuel, Henry. 2012. "A Red Whine from Burgundy." *Daily Telegraph*, November 19.

Savage, Mike, Niall Cunningham, Fiona Devine, Sam Friedman, Daniel Laurison, Lisa McKenzie, Andrew Miles, Helene Snee, and Paul Wakeling. 2015. *Social Class in the Twenty-First Century*. London: Pelican.

Scheiber, Noam, and Patricia Cohen. 2015. "By Molding Tax System, Wealthiest Save Billions." *New York Times*, December 30.

Schielke, Samuli. 2012. "Living in the Future Tense: Aspiring for World and Class in Provincial Egypt." In *The Global Middle Classes: Theorizing through Ethnography*, edited by Rachel Heiman, Carla Freeman, and Mark Liechty, 31–56. Santa Fe, NM: School for Advanced Research Press.

Schor, Juliet. 1999. *The Overspent American: Why We Want What We Don't Need*. New York: HarperPerennial.

Sherman, Rachel. 2017. *Uneasy Street: The Anxieties of Affluence*. Princeton, NJ: Princeton University Press.

Shim, Elizabeth. 2013. "Image Industry Weds Korea Cool to China's New Rich." Associated Press, August 13.

Shotter, James. 2013. "Richemont Defies China Fears." *Financial Times*, April 24.

Skeggs, Beverly. 1997. *Formations of Class and Gender*. London: Sage.

Smith, Daniel. 2016. *Elites, Race, and Nationhood: The Branded Gentry*. London: Palgrave.

Smith Maguire, Jennifer. 2017. "Wine and China: Making Sense of an Emerging Market with Figurational Sociology." In *The Social Organisation of Marketing: A Figurational Approach to People, Organisations, and Markets*, edited by John Connolly and Paddy Dolan, 31–59. Basingstoke, UK: Palgrave Macmillan.

Smith Maguire, Jennifer, and Ming Lim. 2015. "Lafite in China: Media Representations of 'Wine Culture' in New Markets." *Journal of Macromarketing* 35, no. 2: 229–42.

Spence, Emma. 2016. "Performing Wealth and Status: Observing Super-Yachts and the Super-Rich in Monaco." In *Handbook on Wealth and the Super-Rich*, edited by Iain Hay and Jonathan V. Beaverstock, 287–301. Cheltenham, UK: Edward Elgar.

Sun, Yuanqing. 2016. "Aiming to Go Global." *China Daily*, July 22.

Thompson, E. P. 1978. "Eighteenth-Century English Society: Class Struggle without Class?" *Social History* 3, no. 2: 133–65.

Tompson, Christopher. 2014. "No Easy Money to Be Made from Shoppers." *Financial Times*, May 5.

Trebay, Guy. 2016. "In Milan, Ermenegildo Zegna and Ralph Lauren Zero In on the One Percent." *New York Times*, January 18.

Vallance, Charles, and David Hopper. 2013. *The Branded Gentry: How a New Era of Entrepreneurs Made Their Names*. London: Elliot and Thompson.

Vandervelde, Mark. 2016. "Hugo Boss Chief Exits after Profit Warning." *Financial Times*, February 26.

Veblen, Thorstein. (1899) 1959. *The Theory of the Leisure Class: An Economic Study of Institutions*. New York: Viking.

Vogel, Carol. 2012. "This Little Rothko Went to Market." *New York Times*, November 4.

Vogel, Carol. 2013a. "Before the Gavel Falls, It's All Free to Look At." *New York Times*, May 3.

Vogel, Carol. 2013b. "Like Half the National Gallery in Your Backyard." *New York Times*, April 21.

Wealth-X. 2017a. *Billionaire Census 2017*. New York: Wealth-X Applied Wealth Intelligence.

Wealth-X. 2017b. *UHNW Interests, Passions, and Hobbies Study*. New York: Wealth-X Applied Wealth Intelligence.

Weinland, Don, and Laura Noonan. 2016. "Private Banks Woo China's Rising Billionaires." *Financial Times*, September 12.

Wilson, Peter. 1973. *Crab Antics: The Social Anthropology of English-Speaking Negro Societies of the Caribbean*. New Haven, CT: Yale University Press.

Wood, Helen, and Beverly Skeggs, eds. 2011. *Reality Television and Class*. London: Palgrave.

Xie, Yu. 2014a. "Foreign Banks Retooling Products for the New Chinese Rich." *China Daily*, January 3.

Xie, Yu. 2014b. "Sailing into the Future China-Style." *China Daily*, January 9.

Xu, Kangping. 2016. "Smart Age Makes a Billionaire in Six Years." *China Daily*, April 18.

Yen, Hope. 2013. "Rising Riches: One in Five in US Reaches Affluence." Associated Press, December 9.

Zhu, Ping. 2014. "What's the Best Way to Protect Wildlife?" *China Daily*, August 14.

Jennifer Smith Maguire is professor in the Sheffield Business School, Sheffield Hallam University. Her research focuses on processes of cultural production and consumption in the construction of markets, tastes, and value.

IS CONTEMPORARY LUXURY MORALLY ACCEPTABLE?

A Question for the Super-Rich

Joanne Roberts

Abstract This article investigates the moral acceptability of contemporary luxury. The meaning of luxury and its manifestations in today's economically developed countries are explored. The nature of morality is considered, and the evolving moral standing of luxury from the classical period to modern times is reviewed. Based on an elaboration of the significant positive and negative consequences of the production and consumption of luxuries, the moral standing of contemporary luxury and the questions it raises for the super-rich are discussed. The author argues that the moral standing of contemporary luxury is dependent on the social and economic context within which it is situated. This is because the meaning of both luxury and morality vary according to social context. Further, where luxury divides and stimulates degenerate, unethical, and criminal activities, it is morally indefensible; but where luxury unites community and advances human endeavor, it can be defended on moral grounds. However, in the contemporary period, growing economic inequality is increasingly overshadowing any positive moral impact of luxury.

Keywords luxury, inequality, morality, super-rich

Today luxury is ubiquitous in economically developed countries where one can indulge in the consumption of a luxury scone in a high street café while browsing a luxury holiday brochure or pass by a luxury property development on the way to a luxury flagship store. Yet, just over a century ago, significant portions of the populations of these countries lived in extreme poverty (Ravallion 2016: 15), and only a small elite had the means to indulge in luxurious lifestyles.

Cultural Politics, Volume 15, Issue 1, © 2019 Duke University Press
DOI: 10.1215/17432197-7289486

The prevalence of prosperity arising from economic growth in the post-1945 period, accompanied by a decline in levels of inequality due to the adoption of policies that worked to redistribute income and wealth, and to promote social mobility in these countries, led to a growing demand for luxuries. When economies are expanding, individuals may share the benefits arising from wealth creation through improved standards of living and increased consumption of goods and services. Once basic needs are fulfilled, the individual's consumption often turns to luxuries, such as designer clothes, gourmet restaurant meals, secluded holiday resorts, and high-performance cars. The acquisition of luxury goods and services is frequently seen as a realization of the expectations of continuous economic progress, while the desire to consume such goods and services can act as an incentive for the hard work, entrepreneurial endeavor, and innovation on which economic growth depends. Yet when economic growth slows, stops, and even becomes negative, its impact is not shared by all. The poor in the economically developed countries have been hit the hardest by the global financial crisis of 2008 and the austerity measures that governments have adopted in its aftermath, whereas the wealthy have benefited from tax cuts and favorable investment opportunities. Hence a feature of these countries in the contemporary era is that, despite the reduction of inequality during the post-1945 period, most people are now experiencing declining incomes in real terms, while the top 1 percent continue to prosper (Stiglitz 2013; Dorling 2014; Piketty 2014).

Although the richest 1 percent of the world's population own more wealth than the whole of the rest of humanity (Credit Suisse 2017: 156), there is great diversity among this 1 percent of individuals, from the merely affluent to multibillionaires. High net worth individuals (HNWIs), that is, those with investible wealth of US$1 million or more, numbered 16.5 million globally in 2016, and they held total wealth of US$63.5 trillion (Capgemini 2017: 7).[1] For the purposes of this article, this 0.22 percent of the global population is referred to as the super-rich.

Since financial wealth can attract higher returns than the general rate of economic growth (Piketty 2014), the preservation and escalation of the privileged economic position of the super-rich is assured. Consequently, Thomas Piketty (2014) argues, we are returning to a form of patrimonial capitalism dominated by inherited wealth that was typical in the Belle Epoque. This view is supported by the finding that, over the next twenty years, five hundred people will hand over $2.1 trillion to their heirs (UBS/PWC 2016: 6). In such a context, the promise of growing incomes and wealth through hard work facilitated by social mobility becomes hollow (Littler 2017). This growing inequality threatens social stability and democratic values. Moreover, 10 percent of the world's population live in extreme poverty, surviving on less than 1.90 international dollars per day (Roser and Ortiz-Ospina 2017).[2]

Consequently, it is in the contemporary era of economic uncertainty, widespread austerity, and growing inequality that I want to question the moral acceptability of luxury. I will argue that the moral standing of contemporary luxury is dependent on the social and economic context within which it is situated. This is because the meaning of luxury and morality vary according to social context. Nevertheless, luxury does raise fundamental ethical questions in the face of widespread poverty and human suffering.

Hence the question posed in this article must be addressed to the super-rich who endorse the global neoliberal system, which enhances their own wealth while simultaneously promoting greater inequality through low taxation and the rolling back of the state and redistributive policies (Beaverstock, Hubbard, and Short 2004; Wilkin 2015).

The article begins by exploring the meaning of luxury and how it is manifested in the economically developed countries of the contemporary era. The nature of morality is then briefly considered, and the evolving moral standing of luxury from the classical period to modern times is reviewed. The significant positive and negative consequences of the production and consumption of luxuries are subsequently elaborated as a basis for a discussion of the moral standing of contemporary luxury and the questions it raises for the super-rich.

Luxury: From an Idea to Contemporary Manifestations

Luxury is often defined in terms of rare, refined, and expensive products and services of the highest quality as well as associated with a rich, comfortable, and sumptuous lifestyle. It is also viewed as unnecessary, superfluous, or an indulgence. Yet luxury can also be used to describe what Juliana Mansvelt, Mary Breheny, and Iain Hay (2016) call "life's little luxuries," such as eating a box of chocolates while watching a film on a Saturday evening. For those with busy lives, quality time of one's own or shared with loved ones can be a luxury. Luxury is, then, more than a term to describe a group of objects or services; rather, it is an idea.

In his seminal contribution, *The Idea of Luxury*, Christopher J. Berry (1994) provides a detailed historical exploration

of luxury and defines it as the antonym of necessity, in that it is distinct from basic needs, which are nonintentional and universal. For Berry, luxury occupies the realm of wants and desires. Yet he also argues that luxuries must be the object of socially recognized desire and, as such, capable of giving pleasure rather than merely relieving pain. What is clear from Berry's analysis is that luxury cannot be objectively defined because it depends on cultural, social, and individual contexts and meanings. Moreover, goods and services that may be regarded as socially unnecessary by some may be "needed" by others, either in a specific instrumental sense or because they are the object of intense desire (i.e., psychologically necessary) or intense identification (e.g., cherished objects). Hence Berry defines luxuries as "those goods that admit of easy and painless substitution because the desire for them lacks fervency" (41). Consequently, not all unnecessary goods or services are luxuries to everyone. Even the conspicuous consumption identified by Thorstein Veblen (1899) in the late nineteenth century may be based on necessity rather than desire if it is required for individuals to maintain their social status.

Of course, this definition differs from that offered by those exploring luxury from a business perspective. So, for instance, Michel Chevalier and Gérald Mazzalovo (2012) argue that a luxury product must have a strong artistic content, be the result of craftsmanship, and be international. Luxury has also been classified in terms of its accessibility. For example, Danielle Allérès (1990) identifies three levels of luxury: inaccessible—exclusive unique items; intermediate—expensive replicas of unique items; and accessible—factory produced in large production runs. In the contemporary era, we are also witnessing a proliferation of terms such as *new luxury* or *mass luxury*. For Jean-Noël Kapferer and Vincent Bastien (2012), this is the result of the efforts of traditional brands to trade up as well as luxury businesses offering products and services to a wider global market in their drive for profits. Such changes also reflect the fragmentation of the production process, such that the design process may involve significant artistic inputs and craftsmanship but the final luxury goods and services can be mass produced in low-cost locations without any loss of quality (Thomas 2007). Customers have also engaged in trading up in certain areas while trading down in others (Silverstein and Fiske 2003). In this way, savings on the cost of basic goods sourced from discount stores like Walmart and Primark can be diverted to the purchase of high-quality superfluous goods and services.

The democratization of luxury (Kapferer and Bastien 2012), characterized by the shift to mass luxury, has been accompanied by the emergence of the idea of meta-luxury (Ricca and Robins 2012) and über luxury (Quintavalle 2013) to distinguish between mass-produced luxuries and those luxuries that remain exclusive, often because they are rare or the result of high levels of skill and craftsmanship, and their cost renders them accessible only to the super-rich. Examples of such luxuries include bespoke tailoring, haute couture, and individually designed items from jewelry to private jets and yachts.

In the contemporary economically developed countries, the idea of luxury is overwhelmingly associated with the luxury goods and services available in local and global markets. It is this market manifestation of luxury with which this article is concerned when assessing the moral acceptability of contemporary luxury. However, before progressing, it is important to briefly consider the moral standing of luxury and how this has evolved up to the contemporary period. To do this, it is necessary to begin by briefly elaborating on the meaning of the term *morality*.

The Moral Standing of Luxury
What Is Morality?

The nature of morality is a core philosophical question that has stimulated much reflection and debate among philosophers from the times of Socrates and Aristotle to the present day. The field of moral philosophy is concerned with ethical questions concerning what is right and wrong, good and evil, vice and virtue. According to dictionary definitions, *morality* refers to the quality of being moral, where moral is concerned with human behavior; to be moral one must conform to conventional accepted standards of conduct.[3] Because a full discussion of the nature of morality is beyond the scope of this article, attention here focuses on understandings that will assist our evaluation of the moral standing of contemporary luxury.

The terms *morality* and *ethics* are often used interchangeably. However, there is an important distinction to be made between the moral and the ethical. As Paul Weiss (1942: 381) notes, "[A] man is *moral* if he conforms to the established practices and customs of the group in which he is. He is *ethical* if he voluntarily obligates himself to live in the light of an ideal good." Furthermore, according to Bernard Gert and Joshua Gert (2017), the term *morality* can be used in two ways: first, descriptively, to refer to certain codes of conduct put forward by a society or a group or accepted by an individual for his or her own behavior; second, normatively, to refer to a code of conduct that, given specified conditions, would be put forward by all rational persons. The latter suggests that what is right and what is wrong or what is ethical are universally understood.

Moral behavior is central to the development of a civilized society because it is necessary to have conventions and standards of conduct to promote cooperation and communication. Indeed, we must act as we would have another act were he or she in our place and vice versa. This requirement of a civilized society is captured in the golden rule: "Do unto others as you would have them do unto you." This rule is found in every society and religion (Weiss 1942; Stace 1937). Moreover, there are incentives to acting in a moral fashion, in the sense that good acts may result in virtuous feelings and praise, while immoral acts give rise to guilt and disapprobation. The actions of individuals are also regulated by the threat of legal sanctions if laws are disobeyed.

The relationship between the fields of law and morality is considered by Steven Shavell (2002), who argues that their observed and optimal domains are in rough alignment with one another. Morality applies as a means of control over much of our social interaction, but law and morality work together to control criminal activities that are not only illegal but also considered immoral. The law on its own applies to a range of activity for which there is no significant moral concern, such as a minimum capital requirement that must be met for a company to be allowed to sell securities on an equity market (Shavell 2002: 228–29). Changes in moral codes over time can stimulate the introduction of new laws. Similarly, the introduction of specific laws can influence what is regarded as acceptable from a moral standpoint.

In this article, the term *morality* is understood as socially constructed such that to act in a moral fashion one must conform to certain standards of behavior within a society or group. Hence what is morally acceptable today may not be so in a different society, group, or era. For example, owning slaves was morally acceptable in the United Kingdom and the United States until the abolition of slavery in the eighteenth and nineteenth centuries, respectively; yet, today, evidence of migrants, en route to Europe from African countries, being auctioned off as slaves in Libya is morally repugnant to most UK and US citizens (Elbagir et al. 2017). Consequently, when considering whether contemporary luxury is morally acceptable, it is necessary to explore this question within a society or group, or from the perspective of the individual consuming luxury within a specific historical period. History reveals that different groups and societies have, over time, taken different moral positions toward luxury.

The Moral Standing of Luxury from the Classical Period to the Present Day

Scholars have traced the changing moral standing of luxury from philosophical, theological, social, political, and economic perspectives from the classical period to the present day (Berry 1994; Adams 2012; Sekora 1977; Cloutier 2015; Sombart [1913] 1967). Prior to the modern era, luxury was viewed as morally dubious, corrupting, and a serious ethical failing. As William H. Adams (2012: 7–8) notes, luxury as "luxus" in classical Latin implied effeminate sensuality, a passion for splendor and pomp, and "luxuria" indicated excess, extravagance, and moral weakness. According to the classical view, if left unchecked, the consumption of luxury could lead to the demise of individuals and the fall of empires. From a Christian perspective, the fall of Adam and Eve can be linked to the indulgence of consuming the apple from the tree of knowledge (Sekora

1977: 44). Furthermore, accounts of the Ancient Greek and Roman empires attribute their decline in part to luxury (Adams 2012: 46–47). The failure to control the consumption of riches acquired through conquest can result in moral failings, ultimately leading to the decline and collapse of an empire.

Despite its morally dubious standing throughout the classical and early modern eras, luxury prospered among the elite and religious leaders. Luxury was acceptable from a Christian viewpoint when it was used to glorify God. The wealth accumulated by the Catholic Church through the sale of indulgences[4] in the early modern era, for example, was spent on expensive works of art and magnificent churches and cathedrals while its leaders, including God's representative on earth, the Pope, lived in great comfort in lavishly furnished palaces. Similarly, sovereigns and their royal courts lived extravagantly, with luxury goods used to displaying their power (Berg 2005: 38).

Nevertheless, until the seventeenth century, access to luxury was controlled by sumptuary laws that regulated and reinforced social hierarchies and morals through restrictions on the consumption of certain types of goods, including clothing and food (Ribeiro 1986: 21–22). The reservation of certain fabrics and ornamentation for certain social orders was intended to provide clear distinctions between social ranks, thereby preserving the social hierarchy (Berry 1994: 31). Consequently, sumptuary laws ensured that money alone could not secure high status in society.

The view of luxury as morally questionable continues today, but its influence has been significantly eroded. The sociocultural, religious moral position on luxury was superseded by the ascendance of an economic and secular standpoint that

emerged in the early eighteenth century. Berry (1994) describes this change as the de-moralization of luxury. It was initiated by the contributions of philosophers and political economists, particularly, Bernard Mandeville's ([1724] 1988) *Fable of the Bees*, which extolled the virtues of the wealth of individuals for society as a whole; David Hume's essay, "Of Refinement in the Arts" ([1777] 1987), which praised luxury's widespread benefits for society; and Adam Smith's ([1776] 1981) *An Inquiry into the Nature and Causes of the Wealth of Nations*, which argued that private vice and luxury were important stimulants to the economy. Hence, from the late eighteenth century, luxury took on a positive economic rather than dubious moral role in society as a generator of employment, export income, tax revenue, and economic growth. Indeed, Werner Sombart ([1913] 1967) and Maxine Berg (2005) attribute the industrial revolution to the rise of luxury consumption, beginning in the eighteenth century. It is this de-moralized view of luxury that is prevalent today. However, such a perspective is not without its critics, as a review of the significant positive and negative impacts of luxury in the contemporary era will show.

Significant Positive and Negative Impacts of Contemporary Luxury
The Positive Impact of Contemporary Luxury

The consumption of luxury underpins a €1.2 trillion global market (D'Arpizio et al. 2017: 1) and contributes to welfare through the employment of hundreds of thousands of individuals across the world. The desire to consume luxury remains a motivational force that drives people to work hard and, in so doing, contribute to economic development. In the United Kingdom alone, the luxury sector contributes £32.2

billion to the economy, or 2.2 percent of gross domestic product, directly employs 113,000 people, contributes £5.2 billion to the Exchequer through tax and National Insurance, and generates exports valued at £25 billion (Walpole 2017: 5).

In addition to the direct positive impact of the production and consumption of luxury on, for instance, employment and taxes, the sector has positive indirect influences, through spill-over effects on other parts of the economy, including the promotion of skills and innovations. Furthermore, through its impact on cities, luxury can contribute to the construction of what Mario Paris (2018) calls "prestigious places" by improving the built environment with potential benefits for all, directly through an improved quality of life and through attracting overseas tourists and the consequent creation of jobs in the hospitality and tourism sectors. Additionally, high-quality built environments, including cultural activities and first-rate service infrastructures, are important for locations seeking to attract domestic and overseas investment in a variety of sectors.

Luxury companies improve the environment not only through the presence of quality retail space and the construction of luxury housing and apartments but also through sponsorship of cultural activities and sports events that engender community within society. Communal events are an important means of strengthening cooperation and communication and thereby the fabric of society. In periods of declining government expenditure, luxury companies and their customers are an important source of the funding that is required to preserve the cultural heritage of humanity through support for public galleries, museums, and cultural venues. For instance, the luxury conglomerate LVMH Moët Hennessy Louis Vuitton has

had a corporate philanthropy program to supports arts and culture since 1990 (see LVMH, n.d.).

Furthermore, the demand for luxuries facilitates the experimentation that can result in major innovations and new technological developments, the benefits of which can be far reaching. Newly developed products are often luxuries. The demand from early adopters, who have the resources to try expensive new products, helps producers to iron out glitches in product design and to scale up for more cost-efficient production. For example, the development of electric cars benefitted from such early adopters. Although still a luxury for most people, electric cars are becoming more affordable, and they have the potential to generate huge benefits for the environment when they become more widely adopted. Given their affluent customers, luxury companies can be at the forefront of advancing environmentally sensitive and sustainable production. Many luxury companies have well-developed strategies to promote sustainability, which, once proven to be effective, can be adopted more widely in the economy (Armitage, Roberts, and Sekhon 2017).

However, as Joanne Roberts and John Armitage (2015) note, some luxury producers eschew technological change and persist in the use of age-old production methods. Because such methods of production are labor intensive, they are expensive and therefore confined to the purview of luxury producers. Hence the demand for some luxury goods supports the maintenance of traditional craft skills as well as the development of new skills. For example, the luxury company Chanel established its subsidiary Paraffection in 1997 to acquire independent ateliers and thereby safeguard their specialty skills in the fields of embroidery, feathers, shoemaking, buttons, artificial flowers, gold smithing, millinery, knitwear, glove making, and pleat making (Abnett 2014). Without the consumption of luxury, such skills might be lost, to the detriment of human creativity and culture.

Moreover, as H. Sidgwick (1894) argued, the production and circulation of superfluous commodities promotes the appreciation and production of beauty and thereby serves the important social function of advancing culture. Many of the very best cultural and aesthetic contributions arising from the demand for luxury go beyond individual consumption and become lasting resources for humanity, inspiring creativity and civility. National museums like the British Museum or France's Louvre are full of cultural artifacts that were once the luxuries consumed by past generations.

Where luxury results in the unification of communities through, for instance, the development of public access to luxury in the form of public museums and libraries and the enrichment of cultural environments accessible to all, it has a positive moral value (Cloutier 2015). Hume's ([1777] 1987) claim that the growth of luxury has a civilizing and potentially unifying impact in relation to the community and nation with a positive impact on morality is relevant to the contemporary period. However, today, the widespread consumption of luxury, based as it is on significant inequality, also has a negative impact, to which our attention now turns.

The Negative Impact
of Contemporary Luxury

The consumption of luxury can appear wasteful and socially divisive in a period of continuing austerity in the economically developed countries. For instance, when 22 percent of the UK population live in

poverty, including 4 million children (JRF Analysis Unit 2017: 10), it seems obscene to most people that wealthy individuals are willing to pay £279,000 for a rare 2014 Himalaya Birkin Hermès handbag made from Nilo crocodile hide and adorned with eighteen-carat white gold and diamond-encrusted details (Jordan 2018). The widespread adoption of neoliberal economic policies characterized by tax cuts and the decimation of public services, together with increased global economic competition, have amplified inequalities and stifled social mobility since the 1970s (Stiglitz 2013; Dorling 2014; Piketty 2014). This trend was accelerated by the 2008 global financial crisis. Moreover, those with wealth have been able to influence centers of power to ensure that policies and regulation work in their favor (Frank 2008; Wilkin 2015). Such developments not only underpin the rising demand for exclusive luxuries from the super-rich but also drive social fragmentation, to the detriment of society.

Furthermore, the demand for luxury can lead to the wasteful and damaging use of resources. For example, gold mining, with its use of forced and cheap labor and chemicals, especially mercury, and more recently cyanide, is socially and environmentally damaging (Naylor 2011: 26–36). Today, gold extraction methods are being implemented on an industrial scale, giving rise to an ever-increasing pace of environmental degradation. Yet as the destruction of the environment and pressure on sustainability come increasingly into question, there will be a growing necessity for a change in how we view the Earth's resources. Hence the depletion of resources and the imperatives of climate change may force changes in the consumption of luxury. Exploring the case for the re-moralization of luxury, Berry

(2016) argues that it is the impact on the environment and sustainability that is likely, in time, to provide the strongest case for a return to a morally prohibitive view of luxury.

Immoral behavior already arises from the wealth required to sustain luxury consumption. Francesca Gino and Lamar Pierce's (2009: 142) experimental study found that proximity to wealth encourages more frequent cheating than an environment of scarcity. They argue that the presence of abundant wealth provoked feelings of envy toward wealthy others and overstatement of performance, which leads to unethical behavior. Hence faced with super-rich customers, suppliers of luxury goods and services may overstate their value or evidence of their authenticity. R. T. Naylor (2011), for instance, traces the immoral behaviors of those supplying segments of the luxury market as diverse as gemstones, fine art, historical artifacts, fine wines, and Cuban cigars. These behaviors range from theft and smuggling cultural artifacts from war-torn regions such as Syria to misleading consumers who are unable to distinguish between a counterfeit product packaged as an authentic luxury product. As I have argued elsewhere, ignorance in many forms pervades the luxury market (Roberts 2018).

Desire for luxury can lead to immoral and criminal behavior among its suppliers and those wishing to consume it. The inequality required to sustain luxury can lead to crime arising from the desperation of those experiencing extreme poverty or from a desire of those who cannot afford luxury to engage in criminal activity to obtain it. Hence luxury can become a target of crime, as the spate of raids on luxury retailers in UK and US cities during the past few years has demonstrated (Cook 2017). Moreover, the desire of the super-rich to enjoy pristine city spaces with clean streets and immaculate parks influences the policies of governments and can lead to the criminalization of the poor. In 2017, an increasing number of local councils in the United Kingdom were using public space protection orders[5] to fine people sleeping rough in streets and parks. Since most homeless people are extremely poor, the imposition of a fine constitutes criminalization of poverty.

A life of luxury and the desire to maintain it can also lead to immoral behavior. Chrystia Freeland (2013: 239) documents the behavioral changes of those who reach billionaire status and become accustomed to prioritized and high-quality service, noting that they can become impatient and intolerant and even abusive when they receive poor service. Furthermore, studies have revealed that upper-class individuals behave more unethically than lower-class individuals. For instance, Paul K. Piff et al. (2012: 4086) found that upper-class individuals were more likely to break the law while driving, to exhibit unethical decision-making tendencies, take valued goods from others, lie in a negotiation, cheat to increase their chances of winning a prize, and endorse unethical behavior at work than were lower-class individuals. Based on these findings, the authors argue that upper-class individuals' unethical propensities, in part, result from a more favorable attitude toward greed. Recent scandals concerning the financial arrangements of the super-rich would seem to bear out such findings. Evidence from the leaking of the Panama and Paradise papers (Obermaier and Obermayer 2017; Guardian 2017) shows the extent to which the super-rich take advantage of legal advice on how to minimize tax liability through tax avoidance and evasion. While tax avoidance is not illegal, it may be regarded as immoral when it diminishes the resources available to a community, especially in a period of general austerity and decline of public service provision. The use by the super-rich of shell companies in tax havens to protect identity and enhance wealth can also underpin illegal activities, including tax evasion.

The idea that indulgence in luxury can have a negative impact on the individual and society has a long history (Adams 2012; Cloutier 2015; Sidgwick 1894). Too much comfort and excessive consumption of rich food, drink, and stimulants can lead to weakness and ill health through obesity and disease, diminishing the ability of those who indulge in excess to contribute to society. Although evidence suggests that as nations become more prosperous levels of obesity increase, the patterns of obesity within nations are complex (Thompson 2013). The poor diet of those on low incomes is as likely to lead to obesity and ill health as the excessive consumption of fine wine and foods by the wealthy. Moreover, UK statistics reveal that those living in affluent areas have higher life expectancies than those living in poorer regions (ONS 2017). It can be argued that it is the inequality on which the consumption of luxury is based in the current era that has a detrimental impact on the health and welfare of individuals rather than the consumption of luxury itself. The consumption of luxury health services is unlikely to damage individuals, yet if the resources deployed to fund such services were devoted to health services for all, they would no doubt have a greater positive impact at a societal level. Luxury is not a negative if it can be enjoyed by all without a detrimental impact on the environment or sections of society. However, because the contemporary consumption of luxury is underpinned by inequality, its moral standing is brought into question.

Is Contemporary Luxury Morally Acceptable? A Question for the Super-Rich

In addressing the question of whether luxury is morally acceptable in the contemporary era, it is important to recognize that the meanings of luxury and morality are constantly evolving, such that what are regarded as luxury and as morally acceptable today may not be so tomorrow. Additionally, when considering morality, one needs to consider what is morally acceptable within a given society or social group as well as what is ethically acceptable at a societal level. Hence I will focus on the question as it pertains to the super-rich.

There is a strong argument in favor of luxury when it advances culture for humanity as a whole (Sidgwick 1894) by leading to a legacy in terms of cultural artifacts or a lasting change to knowledge or behavior that has a widespread impact beyond the individual luxury consumer. Nevertheless, in contemporary democratic states, one should question whether the super-rich, as the primary consumers of luxury cultural artifacts, should be the arbiters of a society's cultural heritage. Furthermore, the demand for experiential luxury is growing (Euromonitor 2017), and if such consumption has an impact only on the individual consumer, the argument that luxury contributes to cultural heritage loses its moral validity.

Even though the production of luxury may create economic benefits for society, it is necessary to recognize that these benefits accrue disproportionately to the super-rich, who reap the largest share of returns generated in the contemporary neoliberal system. Moreover, if one explores the wider social value of luxury production, one might argue that if the effort employed in its production was spent relieving the pain of those in need of the basic requirements of life, it would produce more happiness (de Laveleye, Armitage, and Roberts 2016). However, whether it is possible to successfully redirect resources from the production of luxury to the production of necessary goods and services is debatable. Nevertheless, studies show that increased luxury consumption does not automatically result in greater happiness (Frank 2008; Frank 2000; Skidelsky and Skidelsky 2012). Indeed, Robert H. Frank (2000) argues that raising taxation to merely moderate the excesses that are evident in contemporary luxury consumer culture can enable an increase in government expenditure that could significantly improve the quality of life for everyone.

A counter to this redistribution argument concerns the need to motivate individuals. If individuals are unable to reap the benefits of their efforts in terms of improvements in the quality of their own lives, will they engage in enterprising and productive activity? Would the resources currently available to be redistributed to a wider society exist without the incentives of individual betterment? Also, while the motivations of those who have achieved their positions of privilege through hard work and enterprise may have benefited society as a whole, it is an open question as to whether those who inherit this wealth will have the same motivations and whether their activities will lead to wider economic benefits. Creating wealth through entrepreneurial activity often depends on firsthand engagement with economic actors ranging from consumers and workers to suppliers and regulatory institutions; however, sustaining and growing wealth can be achieved through arm's-length engagement in the economy, facilitated through financial advisors. Hence the activities of those who inherit

vast wealth may have less benefit to society, and such individuals may be too far removed from the consequences of their decisions to act in a fashion that is morally acceptable to society.

Rather than diminishing the quality of luxury goods and services for a few with the aim of reallocating resources to enhance the life conditions of the many, an alternative approach is to work toward greater quality of goods and services for everyone. The super-rich might argue that this already occurs through the economic growth that luxury stimulates as well as its positive spill-over effects and its contribution to the preservation and advancement of culture and the built environment for the enjoyment of all. However, this view depends on the premise that continuous economic growth is desirable and sustainable. Yet as Tim Di Muzio (2015) argues, this idea is perpetuated by the global neoliberal system and its advocates, namely, the super-rich, despite the threat of environmental collapse that accompanies such growth.

While in a hierarchical authoritarian society luxury is distributed according to one's social position underpinned by economic power, in democratic societies there should be no reason why all individuals should not have the opportunity to enjoy and benefit from luxury. Community luxury in the form of quality public services, including health care, education, libraries, and museums could be provided through higher rates of taxation. Luxury does not have to be morally dubious if it generates benefits for all. As David Cloutier (2015) has argued, when it supports the community, rather than merely the individual, luxury is morally acceptable. In ancient Greece, where the first experiments with democracy occurred, the unifying force of luxury was evident when the meat from animals sacrificed at the Acropolis was distributed among the community (Scott 2012: 33). Today, neoliberal governments fail to engage in such unifying activity as they eschew a more equitable distribution of income and wealth. This leads to a growing inequality between the super-rich and the rest of society, a disparity that was most recently advanced in the United States by President Donald Trump's tax cuts in December 2017.

As government expenditure declines in line with reduced tax revenues, a void in public services grows, which is being partially filled by the philanthropic activities of the super-rich and business corporations, including those in the luxury sector. However, it is important to bear in mind three points in relation to the philanthropy of the super-rich. First, the super-rich actively support the neoliberal economic system that drives down taxes through leveraging their economic power to influence the political system. Second, unlike public expenditure for which democratic governments are accountable to their electorates, the philanthropic choices made by the super-rich and private companies are not accountable to wider society. Third, the tax-deductible nature of charitable donations, for instance to Ivy League universities, can further reduce the tax revenue available to support a government's program to alleviate what it might deem more pressing issues of social deprivation.

Hume's argument for luxury as a promoter of a more cultured society is also brought into question when the scale of inequality stimulates criminal activities on the part of those at the top and bottom of the income distribution. Increasing wealth and the ability to consume luxury does not necessarily lead to more civilized activity in terms of socially responsible behavior.

Rather, inequality, if left unchecked, can lead to increasing and significant social fragmentation as the super-rich pull up the drawbridge of social mobility and focus on protecting and expanding their own wealth.

Of course, the super-rich are aware of their questionable moral position and the impact of their luxurious lifestyles in the face of significant inequality. Although they happily engage in philanthropic activities to support the less fortunate and assuage their own feelings of guilt (Freeland 2013), they have an aversion to addressing inequality and are sensitive about how they are perceived in society. This is exemplified in the criticism leveled at former US president Barack Obama for using terms such as *the rich* or *those at the top* to identify the country's top earners (Freeland 2013: xii). The super-rich view such terms as divisive and as holding an implicit denigration of their success. Such sensitivity is surely a sign of insecurity and an awareness of the moral dilemmas arising from great financial success alongside widespread poverty. This moral dilemma may, in part, account for the growth of inconspicuous or stealth luxury consumption (Faiers 2016) and the increasing demand for security services for the super-rich (Cox 2016).

In a socially fragmented society, common moral norms can disintegrate such that what is morally acceptable to the super-rich diverges significantly from what is morally acceptable to the rest of society. One's moral view of luxury results from one's social position and economic power. Yet there remains a moral position based on fundamental ethics, a normative idea of right and wrong that can be recognized by any rational person. For instance, the treatment of the survivors of London's Grenfell Tower disaster in June 2017, together with the lack of adequate investment in this social housing, which contributed to the spread of the fire at the twenty-four-story apartment block, evoked widespread moral indignation across all sections of the United Kingdom's population. The fire not only killed seventy-one people but also left members of over 320 households homeless (Rawlinson, Sherwood, and Dodd 2017) in Kensington and Chelsea, the wealthiest borough of London, where the empty properties of wealthy people numbered more than fifteen hundred (*Telegraph* 2017). The contrast between the position of the poor and that of the super-rich was brought into sharp relief by this tragedy. The moral injustice of such inequality was evident to all, demonstrating the existence of a unified moral standpoint.

Among their peers the super-rich may be comfortable following a moral code that allows for the excessive consumption of luxury goods and services. However, while the consumption of contemporary luxury is not subject to legal prohibition, its moral acceptability is increasingly questionable, based as it is on growing inequality. The super-rich would be wise to note the increasing social fragmentation arising from inequality and the potential it holds to shatter a fundamental, unified moral position. For while the super-rich are able to insulate themselves from the social deprivation on which their growing wealth depends, their position may not be sustainable. After all, in 2016, the super-rich constituted a mere 0.22 percent of the total global population, and their grip on economic and political power depends on the belief that social mobility and perpetual growth are possible. Once the fallacy of such ideas is widely recognized, the status quo cannot be sustained. Moderating their consumption of luxury and contributing a

greater share of their income and wealth to public resources, for instance, by resisting the use of tax havens and supporting redistributive policies, would go some way to demonstrating that the super-rich seek to preserve a shared fundamental, unified moral position with the wider population.

Conclusion

This article has explored the question of whether contemporary luxury is morally acceptable. Having reviewed the significant positive and negative consequences of the production and consumption of luxury, I have shown that it is evident that its moral acceptability in the contemporary era is intricately linked to the growing inequality of income and wealth. For if everyone could have access to luxury in a sustainable fashion, would it be morally prohibitive? Luxury has both the capacity to unify and divide communities. Where it unites community and advances human endeavor, it can be defended on moral grounds. However, where luxury divides and stimulates degenerate, unethical, and criminal activities, it is morally indefensible. In the contemporary period, the growing inequality of income and wealth is increasingly overshadowing any positive moral impact of luxury. As the eighteenth-century proponent of luxury, Adam Smith ([1776] 1981: 96), acknowledged, "No society can surely be flourishing and happy, of which the far greater part of the members are poor and miserable." Moreover, if left unchecked, the divergence between the moral norms held by the super-rich and the rest of society threatens to undermine a fundamental ethical stance recognized by all. To reverse this contemporary trend, the super-rich need to recognize their responsibilities to society and to a universal moral position that has relevance beyond their own enclosed world of secluded estates and private jets. They need to use their economic and political power to bring about a more equitable society and sustainable economy. Nevertheless, luxury consumption continues to expand as it extends from exclusive items for the super-rich to mass luxury for the aspiring middle classes. A blind eye continues to be turned to the injustices of inequality, while the super-rich ease their consciences with philanthropic acts and, together with the middle classes, continue to indulge in their own guilty pleasures.

Notes

1. Capgemini (2017: 6) divides HNWIs into three wealth bands: "those with US$1 million to US$5 million in investable wealth (millionaires next door); those with US$5 million to US$30 million (mid-tier millionaires); and those with US$30 million or more (ultra-HNWIs)."
2. An international dollar would buy in a country a comparable amount of goods and services that a US dollar would buy in the United States.
3. *Collins English Dictionary*, 2nd ed., s.v. "morality."
4. A payment made to reduce the amount of punishment incurred by the commitment of a sin.
5. Public space protection orders came into existence as part of the Anti-Social Behavior, Crime and Policing Act 2014.

References

Abnett, Kate. 2014. "Paraffection: A Labour of Love." *NJAL Newsletter*, February 24. www.notjust alabel.com/editorial/paraffection-labour-love.

Adams, William H. 2012. *On Luxury*. Washington: Potomac.

Allérès, Danielle. 1990. *Luxe, stratégies-marketing*. Paris: Economica.

Armitage, John, Joanne Roberts, and Yasmin Sekhon. 2017. "Luxury Products and Services and the Sustainable Value Chain: Six Management Lessons from Gucci." In *Sustainable Management of Luxury*, edited by M. A. Gardetti, 259–79. Singapore: Springer.

Beaverstock, Jonathan V., Philip Hubbard, and John Rennie Short. 2004. "Getting Away with It? Exposing the Geographies of the Super-Rich." *Geoforum* 35, no. 4: 401–7.

Berg, Maxine. 2005. *Luxury and Pleasure in Eighteenth-Century Britain*. Oxford: Oxford University Press.

Berry, Christopher J. 1994. *The Idea of Luxury: A Conceptual and Historical Investigation*. Cambridge: Cambridge University Press.

Berry, Christopher. 2016. "Luxury: A Dialectic of Desire?" In *Critical Luxury Studies: Art, Design, Media*, edited by John Armitage and Joanne Roberts, 47–66. Edinburgh: Edinburgh University Press.

Capgemini. 2017. *The Wealth Report 2017*. www .capgemini.com/service/world-wealth-report -2017/.

Chevalier, Michel, and Gérald Mazzalovo. 2012. *Luxury Brand Management: A World of Privilege*. 2nd ed. Singapore: Wiley.

Cloutier, David. 2015. *The Vice of Luxury: Economic Excess in a Consumer Age*. Washington, DC: Georgetown University Press.

Cook, Grace. 2017. "Luxury Retail's War with Organised Crime." *Business of Fashion*, November 24. www.businessoffashion.com /articles/intelligence/luxury-retails-war-with -organised-crime.

Cox, Hugo. 2016. "Safe as Houses: How the Super-Rich Make Their Homes Super-Secure." *Financial Times*, September 7. www.ft.com/content /069be746-6f92-11e6-a0c9-1365ce54b926.

Credit Suisse. 2017. *Global Wealth Databook 2017*. publications.credit-suisse.com/tasks/render /file/index.cfm?fileid=FB790DB0-C175-0E07 -787A2B8639253D5A.

D'Arpizio, Claudia, Federica Levato, Marc-André Kamel, and Joëlle de Montgolfier. 2017. *Luxury Goods Worldwide Market Study, Fall-Winter 2017*. Bain and Company. www.bain.com/Images /BAIN_REPORT_Global_Luxury_Report_2017 .pdf.

de Laveleye, Émile Louis Victor, John Armitage, and Joanne Roberts. 2016. "Luxury Is Unjustifiable." *Cultural Politics* 12, no. 1: 42–48.

Di Muzio, Tim. 2015. "The Plutonomy of the 1%: Dominant Ownership and Conspicuous Consumption in the New Gilded." *Millennium: Journal of International Studies* 43, no. 2: 492–510.

Dorling, Danny. 2014. *Inequality and the 1%*. London: Verso.

Elbagir, Nima, Raja Razek, Alex Platt, and Bryony Jones. 2017. "People for Sale: Where Lives Are Auctioned for Four Hundred Dollars." *CNN*, November 14. edition.cnn.com/2017/11/14 /africa/libya-migrant-auctions/index.html.

Euromonitor International. 2017. *Passport: Luxury Goods: Global Luxury Goods Overview*. London: Euromonitor International.

Faiers, Jonathan. 2016. "Sartorial Connoisseurship: The T-Shirt and the Interrogation of Luxury." In *Critical Luxury Studies: Art, Design, Media*, edited by John Armitage and Joanne Roberts, 177–98. Edinburgh: Edinburgh University Press.

Freeland, Chrystia. 2013. *Plutocrats: The Rise of the New Global Super-Rich and the Fall of Everyone Else*. London: Penguin.

Frank, Robert L. 2008. *Richi$tan: A Journey through the Twenty-First Century Wealth Boom and the Lives of the New Rich*. London: Piatkus.

Frank, Robert H. 2000. *Luxury Fever: Money and Happiness in an Era of Excess*. Princeton, NJ: Princeton University Press.

Gino, Francesca, and Lamar Pierce. 2009. "The Abundance Effect: Unethical Behavior in the Presence of Wealth." *Organizational Behavior and Human Decision Processes* 109, no. 2: 142–55.

Gert, Bernard, and Joshua Gert. 2017. "The Definition of Morality." In *The Stanford Encyclopedia of Philosophy*, Fall edition, edited by Edward N. Zalta. plato.stanford.edu/archives/fall2017 /entries/morality-definition/.

Guardian. 2017. "Paradise Papers." November 6. www.theguardian.com/news/live/2017/nov/06 /reaction-around-world-release-paradise -papers-live.

Hume, David. (1777) 1987. "Of Refinement in the Arts." In *Essays: Moral, Political, and Literary*, edited by E. Miller, 268–80. Indianapolis: Liberty Fund.

Jordan, Dearbail. 2018. "The Handbag That Costs as Much as a House." *BBC News*, March 4. www .bbc.co.uk/news/business-43239037.

JRF Analysis Unit. 2017. *UK Poverty 2017: A Comprehensive Analysis of Poverty Trends and Figures*. Joseph Rowntree Foundation, December 4. www.jrf.org.uk/report/uk-poverty-2017.

Kapferer, Jean-Noël, and Vincent Bastien. 2012. *The Luxury Strategy: Break the Rules of Marketing to Build Luxury Brands*. London: Kogan Page.

Littler, Jo. 2017. *Against Meritocracy: Culture, Power, and Myths of Mobility*. London: Routledge.

LVMH. n.d. "Arts and Culture." www.lvmh.com/group /lvmh-commitments/art-culture/ (accessed October 23, 2018).

Mandeville, Bernard. (1724) 1988. *The Fable of the Bees or Private Vices, Publick Benefits*. Edited by F. B. Kaye. 2 vols. Indianapolis: Liberty Fund.

Mansvelt, Juliana, Mary Breheny, and Iain Hay. 2016. "'Life's Little Luxuries?' The Social and Spatial Construction of Luxury." In *Critical Luxury Studies: Art, Design, Media*, edited by John Armitage and Joanne Roberts, 88–107. Edinburgh: Edinburgh University Press.

Naylor, R. T. 2011. *Crass Struggle: Greed, Glitz, and Gluttony in a Wanna-Have World*. Montreal: McGill-Queen's University Press.

Obermaier, Frederik, and Bastian Obermayer. 2017. *The Panama Papers: Breaking the Story of How the Rich and Powerful Hide Their Money*. London: Oneworld.

ONS. 2017. "Statistical Bulletin: National Life Tables, UK: 2014 to 2016." Office of National Statistics. www.ons.gov.uk/peoplepopulationand community/birthsdeathsandmarriages/life expectancies/bulletins/nationallifetablesunited kingdom/2014to2016.

Paris, Mario, ed. 2017. *Making Prestigious Places: How Luxury Influences the Transformation of Cities*. London: Routledge.

Piff, Paul K., Daniel M. Stancato, Stéphane Côté, Rodolfo Mendoza-Denton, and Dacher Keltner. 2012. "Higher Social Class Predicts Increased Unethical Behaviour." *PNAS* 109, no. 11: 4086–91.

Piketty, Thomas. 2014. *Capital in the Twenty-First Century*. Cambridge, MA: Harvard University Press.

Quintavalle, Alessandro. 2013. "Über Luxury: For Billionaires Only." In *Global Luxury Trends*, edited by J. Hoffmann and I. Coste-Maniere, 51–76. Basingstoke, UK: Palgrave Macmillan.

Ravallion, Martin. 2016. *The Economics of Poverty: History, Measurement, and Policy*. New York: Oxford University Press.

Rawlinson, Kevin, Harriet Sherwood, and Virkram Dodd. 2017. "Grenfell Tower Final Death Toll: Police Say Seventy-One Lives Lost as Result of Fire." *Guardian*, November 16. www.theguardian.com/uk-news/2017/nov/16/grenfell-tower-final-death-toll-police-say-71-people-died-in-fire.

Ribeiro, Aileen. 1986. *Dress and Morality*. London: B. T. Batsford.

Ricca, Manfredi, and Rebecca Robins. 2012. *Meta-luxury: Brand and the Culture of Excellence*. London: Palgrave Macmillan.

Roberts, Joanne. 2018. "Luxury and Ignorance: From 'Savoir Faire' to the Unknown." *Luxury: History, Culture, Consumption* 5, no. 1: 21–41.

Roberts, Joanne, and John Armitage. 2015. "Luxury and Creativity: Exploration, Exploitation, or Preservation?" *Technology Innovation Management Review* 5, no. 7: 41–49.

Roser, Max, and Esteban Ortiz-Ospina. 2017. "Global Extreme Poverty." Our World in Data. ourworldindata.org/extreme-poverty/.

Scott, Michael. 2012. "Dr. Michael Scott." Interviewed by Manfredi Ricca and Rebecca Robins at Darwin College, University of Cambridge. In *Meta-luxury: Brand and the Culture of Excellence*, by Manfredi Ricca and Rebecca Robins, 30–36. London: Palgrave Macmillan.

Sekora, John. 1977. *Luxury: The Concept in Western Thought, Eden to Smollett*. Baltimore: John Hopkins University Press.

Shavell, Steven. 2002. "Law versus Morality as Regulators of Conduct." *American Law and Economics Review* 4, no. 2: 227–57.

Sidgwick, H. 1894. "Luxury." *International Journal of Ethics* 5, no. 1: 1–16.

Silverstein, Michael J., and Neil Fiske. 2003. *Trading Up*. New York: Penguin.

Skidelsky, Robert, and Edward Skidelsky. 2012. *How Much Is Enough? Money and the Good Life*. London: Penguin.

Smith, Adam. (1776) 1981. *An Enquiry into the Nature and Causes of the Wealth of Nations*. Indianapolis: Liberty Classics.

Sombart, Werner. (1913) 1967. *Luxury and Capitalism*. Translated by W. R. Dittmar. Ann Arbor: University of Michigan Press.

Stace, Walter T. 1937. *The Concept of Morals*. New York: MacMillan.

Stiglitz, Joseph E. 2013. *The Price of Inequality*. London: Penguin Books.

Telegraph. 2017. "Wealthy Owners of Empty Homes in Grenfell Borough Revealed after Council Blunder." August 2. www.telegraph.co.uk/news/2017/08/01/owners-empty-homes-kensington-chelsea-revealed/.

Thomas, Dana. 2007. *Deluxe: How Luxury Lost its Lustre*. London: Penguin.

Thompson, Derek. 2013. "The Messy, Messy Relationship between Income (and Race) and Obesity." *Atlantic*, November 13. www.theatlantic.com/business/archive/2013/11/the-messy-messy-relationship-between-income-and-race-and-obesity/281434/.

UBS/PWC. 2016. *Billionaires Insights: Are Billionaires Feeling the Pressure?* uhnw-greatwealth.ubs.com/media/8616/billionaires-report-2016.pdf.

Veblen, Thorstein. 1899. *The Theory of the Leisure Class: An Economic Study in the Evolution of Institutions*. London: Macmillan.

Walpole. 2017. *Thriving after Brexit: The Impact of Leaving the EU on the UK's Luxury Goods Sector and Policy Recommendations*. London: Walpole.

Weiss, Paul. 1942. "Morality and Ethics." *Journal of Philosophy* 39, no. 14: 381–85.

Wilkin, Sam. 2015. *Wealth Secrets of the One Percent: The Truth about Money, Markets, and Multi-Millionaires*. London: Sceptre.

Joanne Roberts is professor of arts and cultural management and director of the Winchester Luxury Research Group at Winchester School of Art, University of Southampton. Her research interests include knowledge, innovation, creativity, and luxury. She is the coeditor, with John Armitage, of *Critical Luxury Studies: Art, Design, Media* (2016).

Figure 1 *Hunting Season (Mother & Daughter)*, 2016. Charcoal, pastel, and pencil on paper, 59 × 70½ in. © Toyin Ojih Odutola. Courtesy the artist and Jack Shainman Gallery, New York.

RESISTING the SINGULAR NARRATIVE

Toyin Ojih Odutola

With an introduction by Deborah Frizzell

Toyin Ojih Odutola (b. 1985, Ife, Nigeria) makes enigmatic life-size drawings in charcoal, pastel, and pencil, rendering figures within implied pictorial narratives often set against backdrops of luxury and leisure. While the work is informed by her personal journey of having been born in Nigeria, then immigrating and settling into American culture in conservative Alabama, she deploys an array of sources drawn from art history to popular culture, literature to hashtag research. The nuanced details of the "worlds" surrounding her subjects form a kind of topographical map embracing the figures' bodies, clothes, and accessories in colorful, intricate patterns and textures. Pictorial spaces are subtly distorted, often distended at odd angles, and linear perspective may suddenly flatten out. Pastels are finessed with her fingertips making background landscapes appear like fabrics and fabric folds read like terrain, while her figures' black skin becomes a living landscape of shimmering richness with delicate sheen, varied tonalities and textures. Presented and scaled as grand-manner, historic narratives of the super-rich, this series features Ojih Odutola's imaginative fictions. The artist is conceptually and aesthetically experimenting, stretching the

Cultural Politics, Volume 15, Issue 1, © 2019 Duke University Press
DOI: 10.1215/17432197-7289500

Figure 2 *The Marchioness*, 2016. Charcoal, pastel, and pencil on paper, 77½ × 50½ in. © Toyin Ojih Odutola. Courtesy of the artist and Jack Shainman Gallery, New York.

boundaries of representing blackness, and questioning the contemporary mania of wealth and glamor, structures of class and value, notions of gender, and formulaic traditions of representation. The artist's drawings appear matter-of-fact, and yet the play of space, form, and color may create discomfiting undercurrents that provoke questions about the viewer's own perceptions and experience.

Ojih Odutola is a visual storyteller who layers possible meanings and allusions as conceptual underpinnings, envisioning a world in which blackness is not a unilateral or simple signifier of race. Her visual language suggests an imaginary that is compelling, vibrant, and relevant, especially in opposition to the Trumpian worldview. Some of her art historical influences include two nineteenth-century painters of modern life, John Singer Sargent and James Tissot, while contemporary admired artists who expand the parameters of the representation of blackness and "presumed identity" would include Kerry James Marshall, Lynette Yiadom-Boakye, and the late Barkley Hendricks, the master of the depiction of cool. But for Ojih Odutola, the written word, her fictional trilogy, is an impetus to her visual image making. She has created an epic story about two Nigerian families, the UmuEze Amara and the Obafemi: the first of an ancient noble heritage and the second a nouveau riche family enriched via trade and vineyards, echoing colonialist mercantilism and structural economic inequality. The male heirs from each family have fallen in love and married, a fantasy nurtured by the artist in opposition to actual laws in Nigeria, where being gay and marrying is illegal. Aristocracy and the newly rich thus consolidate their wealth, businesses, property, and privilege, and as part of that consolidation they commission portraits in which their

Figure 3 *First Night at the Boarding School*, 2017. Charcoal, pastel, and pencil on paper, 63¾ × 41½ in. © Toyin Ojih Odutola. Courtesy the artist and Jack Shainman Gallery, New York.

Figure 4 *Pregnant*, 2017. Charcoal, pastel, and pencil on paper, 74½ × 42 in. © Toyin Ojih Odutola. Courtesy the artist and Jack Shainman Gallery, New York.

posture, gestures, gaze, and accoutrements signify the aesthetics of wealth and luxury.

Instagram has been a platform for Ojih Odutola to respond to questions and discussions around notions of the artist's intensions: what meanings could we attribute to a fictional Marchioness in white silk pajamas and a full-length fur coat sitting regally in her chair surrounded by her gold-framed art collection displayed on Matisse-red walls? Because the artist deploys allusion and a mix of formal and conceptual strategies, questions arise from viewers about her own experiences and point of view. Below is a text from her posts about her perspectives on representing wealth and display, self-worth and identity, blackness, and spaces of imagination addressing issues raised by a series of articles on the artist in *Vogue* magazine (Felsenthal 2017; Kazanjian 2018; Smith 2018).

Toyin Ojih Odutola

To add, I would like to emphasize a point not fully addressed in the article @voguemagazine: a reason for black excellence as something we strive for should not be due to societal impositions and expectations, but by CHOICE for us to be excellent, because we want to create and do good work, to be better people—for ourselves, by ourselves.

I agree that some might see my comments about wealth not being an equalizer as a statement soaked in privilege. A la, "wealth isn't such a big deal when you have it." I see it and I know. What I have aimed to do with this family series is address the constant pushing towards wealth as the only aim for people to excel—that excellence comes ONLY with that marker, that exhibition and proof, when it shouldn't; and as a society we can

envision, discuss and enact better ways of working towards and expanding that.

I have seen excellence in all class demographics and forms; it can come from all manner of origins and places. What does it say to younger generations if all they see is wealth as a means of being free? THAT is my question. And furthermore, what does it say to young people about where they are at and how they can create wealth by their own definitions and resources of excellence not associated

Figure 5 *The Adventuress Club, est 1922*, 2016. Charcoal, pastel, and pencil on paper, 67½ × 49½ in. © Toyin Ojih Odutola. Courtesy the artist and Jack Shainman Gallery, New York.

Figure 6 *A Grand Inheritance*, 2016. Charcoal, pastel, and pencil on paper, 89 × 60 in. © Toyin Ojih Odutola. Courtesy of the artist and Jack Shainman Gallery, New York.

Acknowledgments
Many thanks to Jim Blasi for the preliminary design. This artist statement is adapted from material originally posted on Instagram at www.instagram.com/p/BleGunKhm0R/.

References
Felsenthal, Julia. 2017. "At the Whitney, a Vision of Africa—Without the Colonialist Meddling." *Vogue*, October 27. www.vogue.com/article/toyin-ojih-odutola-whitney-museum-interview.
Kazanjian, Dodie. 2018. "Reimagining Black Experience in the Radical Drawings of Toyin Ojih Odutola." *Vogue*, July 17. www.vogue.com/article/toyin-ojih-odutola-interview-vogue-august-2018.
Smith, Zadie. 2018. "On the Extraordinary Artwork of Toyin Ojih Odutola." *Vogue UK*, July 13. www.vogue.co.uk/article/zadie-smith-on-toyin-ojih-odutola-artwork.

Toyin Ojih Odutola earned her BA from the University of Alabama in Huntsville and her MFA from the California College of the Arts in San Francisco. She lives and works in New York. Among her exhibition highlights, Toyin Ojih Odutola includes the Whitney Museum of American Art, New York (2017–18); Brooklyn Museum, New York (2016); Contemporary Art Museum St. Louis (2015); Studio Museum Harlem, New York (2015, 2012); Aldrich Contemporary Art Museum, Ridgefield (2013); and Menil Collection, Houston (2012). Permanent collections include Museum of Modern Art, Whitney Museum of American Art, Baltimore Museum of Art, New Orleans Museum of Art, Philadelphia Museum of Art, Princeton University Art Museum, Spencer Museum of Art, and the National Museum of African Art (Smithsonian).

with money and the feelings of self-worth attached to it—without any comparisons to some type of unrealistic, hyperbolic ideal?

I'm not saying our society (in this capitalistic system we are ruled by) isn't full of problems which wealth cannot in many ways help alleviate; however, as an endgame it can be just as much a trap, just as flattening, and a curse when it comes to seeing all the beauty and richness in the world, especially for those who are seeking more enriching, true fulfillment and change.

Much love.—TOO

Figure 7 *A Misunderstanding with the Mistress*, 2016. Charcoal, pastel, and pencil on paper, 79½ × 60 in. © Toyin Ojih Odutola. Courtesy the artist and Jack Shainman Gallery, New York.

The "HAVES" and the "HAVE YACHTS"

Socio-Spatial Struggles in London between the "Merely Wealthy" and the "Super-Rich"

Roger Burrows and Caroline Knowles

Abstract In the decade between 2007 and 2017 London changed fundamentally. This article is about how the actions of the transnational über-wealthy—the "have yachts"—impinged on the life-worlds of the "merely wealthy"—"the haves." As the authors explore the conceptual utility of gentrification as a way of thinking about these seismic urban changes, they conclude that profound socio-spatial changes and new intensities in the financialization of housing, neighborhood tensions, and cultural dislocations are reshaping London as a plutocratic city and the lives of those who live there in historically unprecedented ways. The concept of "super-gentrification," the authors argue, does not adequately frame these circumstances.

Keywords London, urban geography, super-gentrification, plutocrats

Over the last decade the social sciences have responded to the call of Jonathan Beaverstock, Philip Hubbard, and John Rennie Short (2004) to take the "super-rich" more seriously. Now a robust corpus of material across the academy offers conceptual and empirical analyses of the über-wealthy.[1] This article draws on this literature to interrogate a decade of change in the form and functioning of London, the global city most impacted by the actions of contemporary transnational wealth elites (Atkinson 2017; Atkinson, Parker, and Burrows 2017; Minton 2017). The history of London has long been entwined with expansions of financial capital and the

Cultural Politics, Volume 15, Issue 1, © 2019 Duke University Press
DOI: 10.1215/17432197-7289528

machinations of global plutocrats and their more proximate counterparts (Atkinson, Parker, and Burrows 2017; Webber and Burrows 2016; Wilkins 2013). But what has happened in London in the decade since the global financial crisis is without precedent (Atkinson, Parker, and Burrows 2017; Minton 2017). Our analysis begins with August 9, 2007, when the first rumblings of the crisis began to emerge as the French bank BNP Paribas froze $2.55 billion worth of funds, and ends on June 14, 2017, when over seventy people burned to death in Grenfell Tower, a poorly maintained tower block in one of the most affluent districts of London (Atkinson 2017). These two events bookend a decade in which the character of London changed fundamentally, a decade in which it became a city for global capital and not a city designed to meet the needs and aspirations of its residents (Atkinson 2017; Atkinson, Parker, and Burrows 2017; Minton 2017). Our focus here is not on the impact of transnational über-wealth (the "have yachts") on London in general—already scrutinized by Rowland Atkinson et al. (2016) and, especially, Anna Minton (2017)—but on how their actions have impinged on the life-worlds of "ordinary" (Cunningham 2017)—"merely wealthy"—London elites ("the haves"). Neither *gentrification* nor the expanded term *super-gentrification*, as we will show, adequately frames these newly calibrated social relationships or the city transformations of which they are a part.

Transnational Wealth Elites

Basic data on changing patterns of global wealth since 2007 provide a now familiar context. We could contest the quality of the data and quibble over the appropriateness of different modes of operationalization, but the figures are so shockingly

stark that even if they were, by a very significant magnitude, in error, it would not alter the inescapable conclusion that since the beginning of the global financial crisis patterns of global inequality have not just widened, they have done so on such a scale that some commentators have come to view it as a symptom of a fundamental structural fault in neoliberal capitalism (Streeck 2016).

Any number of measures generates similar conclusions. Oxfam's reports from 2010 demonstrate alarming concentrations of wealth (Oxfam 2010, 2016). Whereas in 2010 the wealthiest 1 percent of the global population possessed 44 percent of global wealth, by 2015, and for the first time in history, they possessed over 50 percent, a figure that—at the time of writing—is likely now closer to 52 percent. Second, whereas in 2010 it was calculated that it would take the combined wealth of the richest 388 people in the world to be equivalent to the combined wealth of the poorest 50 percent, by 2013 it was 92, by 2015 it was 61, and by 2016 it was just 42.[2] The richest 42 people in the world possess as much wealth as the poorest 3.7 billion. The financial services industry produces numerous reports all concerned with the distribution of global wealth, often couched in the language of the number of high net worth individuals (HNWIs).[3] The figures are telling. In 2008 there were estimated to be some 8.6 million such people distributed across the globe (Beaverstock and Hay 2016: 5), but by 2016 this figure had increased by almost 92 percent to 16.5 million. The geographical distribution of this population is highly concentrated: 4.795 million in the United States, 2.891 million in Japan, 1.280 million in Germany, 1.129 thousand in China, 579 thousand in France, and an estimated 568 thousand in the United Kingdom (compared to just

362 thousand in 2008) (Capgemini 2018). Some half a million of them live in and around London, in a set of tightly circum- scribed neighborhoods (Burrows, Webber, and Atkinson 2016). London has been, at least until recently, the city of choice for the global super-rich. The most recent "rich-list" produced by the *Sunday Times Magazine* (2018: 7) reveals that London has the greatest number of resident (sterling) billionaires—ninety-three in 2017, compared to New York with sixty-six, San Francisco with sixty-four, Hong Kong with sixty-three, and Moscow with fifty-five.

Super-gentrification?

Contemporary London is a very different city to the one that Ruth Glass and her colleagues analyzed in the 1960s (Glass 1964), and although her concept of gen- trification has, in subsequent years, been discussed ad infinitum,[4] it remains difficult to explore the empirical materials we want to introduce without a brief reiteration of this concept.

The conceptual functioning of this term was explicit in Glass's (1964: xviii) original formulation:

One by one, many of the working class quarters of London have been invaded by the middle classes—upper and lower. Shabby, modest mews and cottages . . . have been taken over, when their leases have expired, and have become elegant, expensive residences. Larger Victorian houses, downgraded in an earlier or recent periods—which were used as lodging houses or were otherwise in multiple occupation—have been upgraded once again. . . . Once this process of "gentrification" starts in a district, it goes on rapidly until all or most of the original working class occupiers are displaced, and the whole social character of the district is changed.

Glass (1964: xix) described the geographies of gentrification in London in the early 1960s as follows:

There is very little left of the poorer enclaves of Hampstead and Chelsea: in those boroughs, the upper-middle class take-over was consol- idated some time ago. The invasion has since spread to Islington, Paddington, North Kens- ington—even to the "shady" parts of Notting Hill—to Battersea, and to several districts, north and south of the river.

The subsequent histories of gentrification's conceptual and operational complexities have been critically curated by Loretta Lees, Tom Slater, and Elvin Wyly (2010, 2013). The controversies, debates, and issues that this concept has invoked over the last half-century are so central to ongoing debates in urban studies that its continued analytic utility has been both forcefully defended (Butler 2007) and, con- troversially, extended to global and plan- etary scales (Lees and Shin 2015; Lees, Shin, and Lopez-Morales 2016). However, it is undoubtedly the case that many of the predictions Glass (1964: xx) made about London have come true:

Any district in or near London, however dingy or unfashionable before, is likely to become expensive; and London may quite soon be a city which illustrates the principal of the survival of the fittest—the financially fittest, who can still afford to work and live there. . . . Thus London, always a "unique city," may acquire a rare com- plaint. . . . London may soon be faced with an *embarrass de richesee* in her central area—and this will prove to be a problem, too.

Previously "dingy or unfashionable" neigh- borhoods of the East End—with Dalston (Davison, Dovey, and Woodcock 2012) as perhaps the paradigmatic instance—have been reshaped through gentrification, alongside other hitherto unlikely neighborhoods south of the Thames (Jackson and Benson 2014). Research detailing continuing displacement of working-class communities by those with more resources continues. There is no doubt that gentrification—as traditionally understood—continues in London in a form that Glass would recognize. But much else has changed. Glass was writing at the apogee of the Keynesian welfare state and would likely find some of the new state-led tactics of class displacement bewildering and brutal (Atkinson et al. 2016; Glucksberg 2016; Minton 2017). She wrote in the context of a rarely articulated assumption that urban development was governed by the Kuznets curve, which held that as an economy grew economic and social inequality would decrease. This broadly held in Britain until around 1979. However, as Thomas Piketty (2014) has so powerfully demonstrated, this association began to disappear when confronted with the combined onslaught of global marketization, deregulation, privatization, individualization, and neoliberal cognitive capture. As patterns of global wealth inequalities took on a shape that was closer to the 1900s than the 1960s, so they have inevitably influenced the form and functioning of urban life: patterns of socio-spatial inequality in London today are very different from those of the early 1960s (Atkinson, Parker, and Burrows 2017; Burrows, Webber, and Atkinson 2016).

The influx of global wealth has impacted London's skyline, its subterranean world, its ambiance, and its political economy (Atkinson, Parker, and Burrows 2017). A detailed geodemographic mapping of the parts of London that most appeal to the über-wealthy (Burrows, Webber, and Atkinson 2016) reveals few

surprises: Chelsea in the south; South Kensington, Knightsbridge, Belgravia, Mayfair, Notting Hill, and Holland Park in the west; and Hampstead, Highgate, and St. John's Wood in the north; plus a few noncontiguous outposts. Some of these areas have always been domains of long-term locally based wealthy elites; others are more recent additions, incorporated through first-wave gentrification.[5] However, it is our contention that most of them are now in the early stages of profound socio-spatial changes. Whether these changes can be incorporated within the framework of gentrification is a moot point (DeVerteuil and Manley 2017; Fernandez, Hofman, and Aalbers 2016; Glucksberg 2016), which we intend to explore.

Early indications that some of the most affluent neighborhoods in London were changing came from one of the original frontiers of gentrification: Islington. A few years before the financial crash of 2008, Tim Butler and Loretta Lees (2007) claimed to be able to identify what they termed super-gentrification[6] in Barnsbury, part of the prestigious N1 postcode within Islington in North London.[7]

For them this concept denoted:

a further process of gentrification . . . occurring since the mid-1990s . . . that includes a significant step change in social class composition and evidence of social replacement (rather than displacement) with a significant transformation in community relations . . . that involves a higher financial or economic investment . . . than previous waves . . . and thus requires a qualitatively different level of economic resource. (469)

Butler and Lees connected super-gentrification with postderegulation developments in the City of London and the emergence of a new elite cadre of highly paid, often Oxbridge or US Ivy League educated, financiers and lawyers who needed easy access to the city and the West End. This particular fraction of the wealthy were, Butler and Lees argued, different "from both the traditional banking and stockbroking elites that live in areas such as Chelsea, St John's Wood and more recently Notting Hill . . . the super wealthy international bourgeoisie living in Mayfair, Park Lane and much of Kensingston . . . [and] . . . the global managers restlessly roaming the world" (470). Their data show that more affluent professionals from the financial sector were replacing traditional gentrifiers. But unlike the working classes of earlier decades who rented these properties, when in a more dilapidated state, they were not being forced to move. Most could take huge amounts of equity out of their properties when they sold them to the new "super-gentrifying cohort" of "upwardly mobile foreigners" (476). They could move to neighborhoods more attuned to their sensibilities and, we assume, create new displacements.

We interpret this as cultural dislocation, with established residents expressing concern that with arrival en masse of ever more wealthy incomers—with "a big increase in foreign accents"—the area was not what it once was. As Butler and Lees point out, "The new super-gentrifiers were talked about in very similar ways to those displaced by an earlier generation of gentrification." One respondent argues, for example, that the new arrivals "want to change things straight away regardless of what's already there." She finds them "very arrogant" and "not friendly or community minded" and argues that "they put nothing into the fabric of the community, only money into the commercial infrastructure rather than their personalities or talents" (476): infrastructures of

consociation and consumption change and new tensions surface in the neighborhood.

In neighborhoods across London similarly complex socio-spatial shifts are intrinsic to the continuous processes of urban reproduction, as more established middle-class residents who embody a habitus at odds with emergent local cultural fields express similar concerns. But is it appropriate to label this "super-gentrification"? Any response to this demands a rehearsal of debates concerning a core aspect of gentrification theory—class.

In all analyses of social class the issues turn out to be more complex than they appear. In its original formulation by Glass, the concept of gentrification was about the spatial displacement of the working class consequent on territorial invasion by the middle classes—upper and lower. This is clearly what happened in Barnsbury's first wave of gentrification, but equally clearly *not* what began a decade ago when Butler and Lees were researching the area. The reason the concept of gentrification (super or otherwise) is still applicable can be only because it is no longer just about the spatial manifestations of struggles between the working and the middle classes. Instead, struggles between more subtle and granular social classes hold sway. Butler (2007: 166) emphasizes this when he quotes Eric Clark (2005: 258):

Gentrification is a process involving a change in the population of land-users such that the new users are of a higher socio-economic status than the previous users, together with an associated change in the built environment through a reinvestment in fixed capital. The greater the difference in socio-economic status, the more noticeable the process, not least because the more powerful the new users are, the more marked will be the concomitant change in the built environment. It does not matter where, it does not matter when. Any process of change fitting this description is, to my understanding, gentrification.

This statement makes clear why we can refer to "super-gentrification." Gentrification is no longer (just) about the working and the middle classes but any form of displacement involving hierarchical differences in "socio-economic status." Butler and Lees (2007) replace big classes with conceptions derived from commercial geodemographics—the Mosaic classification—that allows for more nuanced spatial micro class analysis (Webber and Burrows 2018).

Mosaic allocates every residential address in Britain to a set of mutually exclusive and exhaustive groups and types based on approximately four hundred spatially referenced pieces of data from commercial and official sources. The version of Mosaic used by Butler and Lees (2007) was constructed in 2003 and classifies each of the 1.78 million postcodes in the United Kingdom to 1 of 61 different types nested within 11 different groups.[8] In their Barnsbury sample of seventy-three respondents they were able to assign sixty-nine Mosaic types: thirty-six were classified as Global Connections, eleven as Cultural Leadership, seven as Counter Cultural Mix, two as City Adventurers, eleven as New Urban Colonists, and two were other types. In comparison to the other areas of gentrification in London for which they also had Mosaic data, a far higher proportion of Barnsbury respondents lived in addresses classified as Global Connections or Cultural Leadership—both nested within the most affluent Symbols of Success group. In contrast, the majority in the other types formed the less affluent Urban Intelligence group. This designation referenced

a collection of postcodes that had hitherto functioned as Mosaic's proxy for neighborhoods at different stages of gentrification. Super-gentrification is thus apparent only when we utilize a more nuanced set of socio-spatial cultural class categories or micro-classes (Weeden and Grusky 2012).

Since Butler and Lees's (2006) research, wealth inequalities in London have accelerated dramatically. Does this mean that processes similar to those they describe have extended to neighborhoods even more affluent than Barnsbury? One area we examined with this in mind, and reported on elsewhere (Webber and Burrows 2016), is Highgate "Village" in north London. Highgate has long been very affluent. It now contains a complex mix of affluent households, including celebrities, cultural commentators, politicians, and billionaires. Despite its wealth, Highgate has long displayed a liberal or radical edge, in the past attracting the wealthy with this sensibility. But recent changes in patterns of global wealth have profoundly impacted Highgate's social dynamics.

Two decades ago its Victorian or Edwardian terraced houses were occupied by what the Mosaic classification at the time described as "younger, high-achieving professionals, enjoying a cosmopolitan lifestyle." Many of them worked at the upper end of public service pay scales as civil servants, academics, and surgeons or in legal, accountancy, or architectural practices. With increased house prices this population is being replaced by those employed in international finance capital: senior employees of large-scale professional and advisory businesses in management consultancies, legal services, accountancy, risk management, and investment advice. As Clark (2005: 258) predicts, this replacement manifests itself in a shift in the dominant architectural aesthetic.

Previously, most new owners would scour architectural salvage yards to restore "period features," make limited improvements, upgrade kitchens and bathrooms, install central heating, or create larger living rooms by removing dividing walls. The new owners of these period properties commission high-end designers to undertake often-brutal structural changes, converting older properties into contemporary state-of-the art living spaces.

Owners of successful family businesses occupy Highgate's larger nineteenth-century detached houses, located farther from the village core. But as these houses come onto the market, people who have acquired capital through the sale of tradable financial assets are the most likely to replace them. The locational decisions of this group of über-wealthy are driven by narrower set of considerations than those they replace. Not attracted to Highgate for its community feel but as a location with properties that can be adapted to meet their requirements, in some cases torn down and rebuilt. The growing disparity between the resources of the über-wealthy and the merely wealthy, established Highgate elite is reflected in territorial displacement and wider cultural conflicts. This is especially evident in planning disputes in which clashes between the values of the incoming global elites and more established residents are starkly revealed (Webber and Burrows 2016: 3149–51).

Highgate is certainly affluent, but perhaps closer to Barnsbury in its house prices and in the social status of its residents than it is to neighborhoods where the gentry have traditionally resided. Perhaps we should explore longer established "super-wealthy" London (Wilkins 2013)? A postcode district that has always been unambiguously dominated by the gentry

might provide a better test case: London W8 is such a place (Burrows, Webber, and Atkinson 2016).

London W8: The Heart of the Alpha Territories

Notting Hill Gate bounds W8 to the north, Holland Park to the west, Knightsbridge to the east, and Cromwell Road to the south. Kensington High Street, which transects it, forms its main commercial artery. In 2014 we interviewed twenty-seven people who lived and or/worked in and around the area—sixteen of them established residents—as part of a broader qualitative study of what we called London's Alpha Territories.

The area now post coded W8 is primarily a Victorian creation. Developed on land occupied by the great country houses—Holland House, the Phillimore Estate, and the Estate of Lord Kensington—Kensington was part of the fashionable world gathered around the court of William and Mary at Kensington Palace in the late seventeenth century, at that time some distance from the city. Transformed by Victorian builders, developers like James Freak who built Onslow Square and urban designers like Thomas Wood, it was intended for "persons of good worth and quality" (Walker and Jackson 1987: 17). Kensington architecture declared the benefits of arts and sciences with a mid–nineteenth-century imperialist confidence. Nearby on the Serpentine stood the original Crystal Palace (1851) exhibiting the best in raw materials, decorative arts, machinery, and jewelry in the Great Exhibition. Extending this display, the Victoria and Albert Museum opened nearby (1852), as did the Royal Albert Hall (1871), joining the Royal Geographical Society (1830), which disseminated the benefits of the explorations on which the British Empire was founded.

From the 1840s the canals and railways connecting it to London ended its status as a fashionable suburb and hastened W8's development. The extension of the underground railway to South Kensington and Kensington High Street (1865–69) and the emergence of the department stores such as Harrods (1861) and Harvey Nichols (1850s) and a cluster of stores lining Kensington High Street made it what it is today. A smattering of Victorian creatives (architects, artists, sculptors, and so on), higher government officials, lawyers, and well-placed city financial types lived there, so that by 1902 Charles Booth's *Life and Labour of the People of London* revealed it to be a predominantly wealthy area, with pockets of the poor being "eased" into North Kensington and Earl's Court.

Victorian (and earlier) versions of what much later became W8 linger in the biographies of its long-term residents. Harriet,[9] who first moved into the neighborhood in 1952, was presented as a debutante at court; she "did the season": the royal enclosure at Ascot, the rounds of dinners, balls, luncheons, and coffee mornings young women did at that time. She remembers the old department stores on Kensington High Street. For several years now she has been selling off the lower floors of her house and moving upward until she now lives on the floor below the attic in which she stores the contents of her parents' house. She notes that similar houses on her street sell for £11 million (in 2014), which she, a beneficiary of rising real estate values, thinks "an insane amount of money." However, Harriet is planning to move "because it has become so expensive." It may be, but she already lives there, and this has brought her financial benefit. What does she mean? Her story pinpoints a type of dislocation we want to unravel. These

can be gathered under two connected headings: *shifting social environments* and *feeling out of place*. These two dimensions offer a description of neighborhood cultural change and a sense of recent transformation and displacement from the vantage point of elite longer-term residents.

Shifting social environments result from gradual processes in which longer-term residents leave the neighborhood and wealthier people arrive. A number of the informants in our study provided detailed descriptions of the changes they were living through. Jane describes these changes and their impact on social relationships in her garden square:

I had lovely flat . . . with its own very pretty garden, right on the square, perfect for grandchildren. . . . I was very happy there and was absolutely convinced I would never move . . . my house had always been pretty socially varied but when I moved there . . . it was affluent but it wasn't crazily affluent. So then what began to happen is . . . there was one very affluent man who was very nice, who became typical of what the rest of the area became, he was gay . . . he had homes all over the world, spent about 2 weeks in London a year. . . . So [in 1992] it was beginning to have a kind of sprinkling of wealthy Europeans who used it as a kind of pied-à-terre. . . . Meanwhile, the flat above me was always occupied by someone I knew very well. . . . Then . . . [it] got sold . . . to a developer. The guy who [then] bought the top flat . . . was mega-wealthy; he was worth billions . . . both the neighbor above me and the neighbor beside me changed, and they all . . . started to work on their flats . . . what was very different [from previous neighbors] was that they obviously didn't care less about the people in the rest of the house.

These shifts are about large-scale differences in wealth and the impact of this on neighborhood relationships. Harriet unfolds the street in which she lives in an almost forensic way, providing glimpses of who lives there from the vantage point of her detached assessment of their foibles and (lack of) neighborly conviviality, indicating that she doesn't feel displaced as much as detached from new arrivals. She knows that the banks dominate the neighborhood; they rent properties for their executives, often Americans, or French families wanting to be close to the Lycée Français Charles de Gaulle. The problem, as she sees it, is not that many of them are foreigners but that they are much richer.

Most of the people in this terrace, I would say at least 50 percent of them are from somewhere else. Not English . . . I mean we've got Italians and French and Americans and Germans . . . Iraqis, they're all charming and delightful people, they're all great, but it's just that they all work for big banks . . . and they're all really high up and high flyers. . . . So I guess that's why they're expensive.

The cast of characters she sets before us includes a roster of the displaced as well as newcomers: a "Bernardo's Boy" enriched by his casual long-term property speculation living with a woman who dislikes him; a Middle Eastern couple who have lived there since the 1980s, initially as students; a Swiss-American couple; a smattering of Japanese, including a family in the basement with a boy who plays the piano; a Jewish New Yorker who moved away; a talented woman potter; an old lady at number 7, who "may still be alive"; a Canadian couple, one of whom has a job in Brussels. Harriet strikes the pose of an interested onlooker rather than as someone who is, as she used to be, involved in the neighborhood. This enables her to think about moving: the problem is,

to where? She turns over the options: the locations of family and friends will guide her.

From Jane's analysis we see that the neighborhood has become more cosmopolitan as well as wealthier. It houses "foreigners" who don't participate in the social relationships of the neighborhood and who display what she considers unacceptable behavior: she means littering and overlooking conventions of greeting, oversights that cause friction.

My street—my beautiful square, never used to be like that—was absolutely littered because everybody put rubbish out whenever they wanted. No one went down to the dustbins, they couldn't be bothered, or it was their cleaner. . . . Somebody else picks things up, and in my building nobody ever picked up the junk mail . . . you couldn't open the door but no one would actually bend down, because somebody else does that. . . . "I'm too rich to bend." And it became very, very alien, very strange. You go to the shops and it's full of French people and different people but no English people, and it was as if the pied piper had been.

Wealthier residents from other countries are, as she understands it, making the neighborhood a different kind of place, a place in which longer-term residents either no longer feel at home or, more emphatically, feel out of place.

This is exacerbated by incomers' material relationship with their own homes. Rolling programs of refurbishment, extension, and improvement disrupt neighbors' lives. Jenny, herself a gentrifier from the 1960s, describes a "tidal wave of misery" destroying her family's "peaceful life":

But it's not a case of people buying houses and just redecorating them anymore, it's a whole new culture of get the space as cheap as you can, and let's expand it, let's do basements, let's do side extensions, let's do loft extensions. . . . First of all there's a lot of foreign bankers coming in, so you'd have maybe single people or a young family, and that was okay because people like that you get to meet and you get to meet their kids, they become part of the community. Now it's buy the property, rip it out literally, even if it's just been redone, rip it out, strip it out, glass walls, take the features out, develop it within an inch of its life, put in a basement, never mind it takes six to nine months, and it's upsetting everybody each side. . . . Most people don't talk to their neighbors about what they want to do they just go ahead and do it. . . . The builders moved in, and a demolition notice went up in our hallway, hard hat area . . . from February until July or June they literally tore the building apart. They took up floors, they took every wall down, they took every floor and ceiling out, right up into the roof, without a care to us, . . . they just treated us like shit basically.

Others also complained about the impact of basement digs on the fabric of their house and their lives. Planning regulations control period properties. Unable to build up or out, wealthy house owners must build down. Basement digs, sometimes including indoor pools, game rooms, and staff quarters, can take up to two years to complete.[10] So extensive are some of these digs that mining engineers oversee them. The building of this new subterranean London for the super-rich has been the subject of much comment but, until recently, little systematic investigation (McCarthy and Kilgour 2011). Recent research we have carried out suggests that such developments are emblematic of how London is changing; along with residential high-rise luxury towers—"luxified skies"—sprouting up across the city (Graham 2015) we are

also witnessing an epidemic of "luxified troglodytism."[11]

Extracting data from planning portals for the seven London boroughs of Camden, Hammersmith and Fulham, Haringey, Islington, Kensington and Chelsea, Wandsworth, and Westminster—all localities that cover core "super-prime" London—between 2008 and the end of 2017, we discovered 4,650 basement developments granted planning permission.[12] Hammersmith and Fulham has the greatest number—1,147 over the decade—followed by Kensington and Chelsea with 1,022 and then Westminster with 678. The great majority—80.7 percent (3,753)—of the basements we would classify as standard one-story-deep excavations, but 16.9 percent (785) were large two-story (or the equivalent in volume) constructions, and 2.4 percent (112) could only be described as mega basements—three stories or more deep (or the equivalent in volume). However, this distribution varies significantly across the boroughs. In Kensington and Chelsea 6.6 percent, and in Westminster 5 percent, are mega. No mega basement development is found in Haringey, Islington, or Wandsworth, and only three instances are found in Hammersmith and Fulham.

In Kensington and Chelsea, where W8 is located, basement developments have spread across the whole borough. The roads clustered near Roland Gardens, Roland Way, and Drayton Gardens have a significant number of excavations, but the majority of these are standard developments. Tregunter Road, Harcourt Terrace, the Little Boltons, and Cathcart Road are home to a significant number of large developments. These roads in particular have seen a notable increase in excavations with swimming pools. Indeed, our data suggest that Tregunter Road (in

SW10 but close to W8) is likely the road with the greatest number of excavations granted permission in the last decade; a full twenty-one basements (three of them mega) have been constructed or are in the process of being built. To the east of Kensington Palace, the roads of Kensington Palace Gardens, Palace Garden Mews, and Brunswick Gardens possess a high concentration of mega developments. By way of illustration, here are some summary details of just three of the developments in W8 or close by to it:

- Creation of new two-story basement under entire house. First story: two staff flats, catering kitchen, games room, shower room, WC. Second story: spa, sauna, steam room, server room, wine cellar, storeroom, cinema, shower room, changing room, swimming pool. Detached house.
- Creation of new two-story basement under entire house and part of garden: swimming pool, mechanical room, steam room, sauna, summer clothes storage, void, changing room, winter clothes storage, gym, cinema. Detached house.
- Creation of new three-story basement under entire house and part of rear garden. First story: staff kitchen, two WCs, gym, media room. Second story: staff bedroom, three WCs, family room, family kitchen, guest bedroom, guest kitchen, bathroom. Third story: laundry room, drying room, sauna, steam room, two shower rooms, WC, jacuzzi, plunge pool, pantry, swimming pool with beach. Semidetached house.

The main features of the shifting social environment described by the longer-term residents we interviewed include the arrival of much wealthier residents with different social habits, many of them from overseas; shifts in the character of neighborhood social relationship; and fragile, difficult connections between neighbors. Refurbishment projects such as extensions, basement digs, and other aspects of renewal and upgrading, depending on their intensities and extent, cause particular tensions because of their impact on neighborhood living conditions. In combination these conditions make long-term residents feel that their neighborhood is no longer a place intended for them.

Our interview data suggest that this is about the differences between their lives and the lives of incomers, who, in being vastly wealthier, live rather differently in their state-of-the-art multiple homes in this and other neighborhoods, and in other countries. Many of our interviewees expressed these social differences as a breakdown in "community," by which they mean long-term attachment to the area and to people they consider to be like them. As another resident, Kate, put it, invoking common interest and emotional investment in neighborhood, a "community of chums in the [swimming] pool." From Kate's and Jenny's comments it seems that the community they helped create forty years ago as early gentrifiers is very different from the one they live in today. Kate, now retired, once worked for the BBC and has lived in the area since the 1980s. Her comments stress the importance of public infrastructures like swimming pools in supporting casual neighborhood connection and social mixing.

I swam with my friend next door but one . . . and I got used to all the people in the swimming pool . . . and we met all sorts of people . . . we got a community of chums in the pool. . . . I made friends with several people who owned stalls in the market, I know all sorts of people round here which I wouldn't. . . . It was an incredible social asset, the swimming pool. [But] they closed it. . . . In the meantime we're going . . . to the Jubilee pool where you're meeting another group of chums and some of the old chums from here, and the rest of the people are going to another swimming pool but we're all split, but you don't even know you're making friends and then suddenly you know all sorts of ladies . . . who live in the area . . . all different backgrounds . . . but then they said we're closing it to build . . . flats and an academy. . . . It's a really valuable asset that pool. But of course they said "oh no we're redeveloping you can get lost" type of stuff.

Rising land values, and the pressure this places on spaces that can be further financialized by building expensive apartments, swallow public infrastructures *and* neighborhood connections. Many of the people in our study lamented the loss of corner shops where they could buy "ordinary provisions," and pubs where they could connect with neighbors. In place of these ordinary spaces, art dealers, estate agents, upscale restaurants, and other enterprises able to match rising land values with high rents compose the neighborhood. Expensive apartments and luxury retail operations change the character of the neighborhood.

Another dimension of dislocation concerns the outward appearance of neighborhood properties. New wealthy residents bring signs of a more affluent standard of habitation. Their properties are highly groomed, and their landscape gardening conforms to an aesthetic using particular planters, trees, and shrubs: bay trees clipped into shape; window boxes and front door colors tastefully toned. Windows reveal glimpses of carefully designed interiors. Large disposable incomes, and the expertise they secure, maintain these

aesthetics. Jenny's sense of dislocation is about not having the money to fit in with the changes brought by plutocratic capital to the neighborhood. Her dislocation is about the humiliation of living in a flat that is visibly not maintained to these standards, announcing her modest circumstances to the street.

Shifting neighborhood social and physical environments, the sense of displacement and the feeling of being out of place this engenders, repeat tropes from the gentrification literature already discussed. But taking a closer look at these dislocations, it becomes clear that what is happening in W8 is more intensive with the invasion of plutocratic capital. Here we note the intensification in turning residential property into a financial asset (Fernandez, Hofman, and Aalbers 2016). Every square inch has value. Basements increase square footage and maximize house owners' investment. Homes become financial assets alongside others like shares and art collections. Housing in W8 is a repository of accumulated wealth, a major site of consumption of decor and home reconstruction, and an asset for future generations. As in the eighteenth and nineteenth centuries, houses ground dynastic ambition. Record sums are spent developing new housing and refurbishing older stock. Howard, as an architect specializing in refurbishing period properties in W8, comments on changes in his practice over thirty years:

I suppose the money people spend, it's changed hugely in the time I've been doing it. Originally you were improving the houses, maybe rewiring, putting an extension . . . it sounds the same, but just the actual quality of what's happened and I suppose the expense, and the quality of finishes, and as people become more prosperous and whole type of new people have come into the borough, some of them foreign. Most of our clients actually I still say the majority are British . . . people [who] have done very well in life or whatever. . . . It's . . . doing up houses to the nines, down to every detail, air conditioning, we dig down, put media rooms in the basement . . . maybe £2/£3/£4 million on a single house, and a lot of them are listed buildings, which has its own constraints and problems and interest. One thing that's changed dramatically I think in the last ten to fifteen years, and it's been a big change, is now property is sold . . . on the American system of selling properties by the square foot rather than by the number of bedrooms or bathrooms . . . therefore every square inch you can gain in terms of space adds to the value of the property.

Conclusion

What we have described in W8 are voluntary displacements in which long-term residents—the haves in our title—have the option of releasing equity ramped up by the have yachts—the plutocrats moving into the area. Although they complain about displacement, they substantially benefit from it financially if not culturally, making these dislocations distinctively different from those Glass and others write about. As Jane says: "I woke up one morning and thought well actually I could move. . . . I sold it in three days . . . for a lovely price." The real losers in these neighborhood transformations are those without an equity stake: private renters and social housing tenants. These micro-housing classes are being relocated outside London's most affluent neighborhoods and, in some cases, out of the city entirely (Atkinson et al. 2016; Glucksberg 2016; Minton 2017), driven by a tidal wave of plutocratic capital. This unprecedented homogenization of the city, driven by concentrations of wealth, has made London less socially diverse, as the poor are driven out and the gap between middle-class wages and house prices widens, producing radically new housing geographies.

The processes we describe are forms of gentrification only if we accept Butler and Lees's definition of it as displacements involving hierarchies generative of micro-class distinctions. But, as we have shown, these displacements are of a particular kind. They involve intensified development of homes and neighborhoods through large volumes of capital; they entail a quality and scale of refurbishment and a financialization of domestic space, which is vastly accelerated, if not entirely new, in scope and scale; and they create particular kinds of tensions between neighbors that are about differences in wealth, cultures, consumption, and lifestyle. These changes are producing a new kind of city, a city symbolized in the burned-out carcass of Grenfell Tower and its displaced former residents, abutting the luxury mansions of the plutocrats we have described, with whom they share a neighborhood of parallel universes. The crucial question here concerns urban sustainability and social inequalities—is this really the kind of city in which we want to live? And what moves could be made to undo these developments and their social consequences?

Acknowledgments

This article was written under the auspices of ESRC project ES/K002503/1.

Notes

1. Noteworthy are the essays collected together by Hay (2013) and Hay and Beaverstock (2016), which summarize what is now a large literature. However, it is probably the more recent collection of essays by Forrest, Wissink, and Koh (2017) that provides the most accessible route into this literature for those primarily interested

2. Originally this figure had been calculated to be just eight. However, Oxfam revised the figure as new data became available in January 2018. The details of these revisions can be found in Elliott 2018.

3. HNWIs are usually defined as people holding investable financial assets with a value greater than $1 million. Ultra high net worth individuals (UHNWI) are people with investable assets of at least $30 million.

4. At the time of writing, in May 2018, Google Scholar returns over 109,000 items and Google itself 1.87 million.

5. For example, in the 1960s Notting Hill was a neighborhood that epitomized many of the worst aspects of urban poverty (Pahl 1975). An excellent account of the changing fortunes of the area is provided in the BBC4 TV series *The Secret History of Our Streets* (BBC4 2013).

6. A term originally deployed by Lees (2003) to describe what was happening in Brooklyn Heights, New York.

7. Barnsbury stretches from Upper Street in the east, north toward Holloway Road, westward to York Way and Caledonian Road, and south to Angel. Grand terraces and squares were built in the area from 1820 onward. However, with the extension of the railways, Barnsbury's population of prosperous tradesmen and professionals moved out. After 1945 whole streets were demolished, many replaced with council estates. From the 1960s onward Barnsbury experienced the first wave of classic gentrification of the surviving terraces and squares as described by Glass (1964).

8. See Webber and Burrows (2018, chap. 5) for a discussion, and tables showing this classification.

9. All interviewees have been assigned appropriate pseudonyms.

10. See, for example, the 2015 BBC documentary *Millionaire Basement Wars* (BBC 2015).

11. It sometimes seems as if the super-rich cannot bear to be on the same ground as the rest of us: if they are not in their penthouses atop the luxified skies looking down, they are even higher up still—in their private jets, helicopters (Budd 2016), or even in their own spaceships (Seife 2014); or else they are far out at sea—beyond most jurisdictions—in their "super yachts" (Spence 2017), on their private islands (Urry 2013), or at their very own "seasteads" (Steinberg, Nyman, and Caraccioli 2012); or, of course, and our focus here, they are going underground—living in deep subterranean spaces but still not in the same plane as the rest of us. Thanks are due to Will Davies for this insight.

12. Thanks are due to Sophie Baldwin, Beth Holroyd, and Joseph Nettleton Burrows for carrying out the bulk of this work, which was carried out in collaboration with the *Guardian* (Batty, Barr, and Duncan 2018). Full details can be found in Baldwin, Holroyd, and Burrows, forthcoming.

References

Atkinson, Rowland. 2017. "London, Whose City?" *Le monde diplomatique*, July. mondediplo.com /2017/07/06london.

Atkinson, Rowland, Roger Burrows, Luna Glucksberg, Hang Kei Ho, Caroline Knowles, and David Rhodes. 2016. "'Minimum City'? A Critical Assessment of Some of the Deeper Impacts of Super Rich on Urban Life." In Forrest, Wissink, and Koh 2017: 253–72.

Atkinson, Rowland, Simon Parker, and Roger Burrows. 2017. "Elite Formation, Power, and Space in London." *Theory, Culture, and Society* 34, nos. 5–6: 179–200.

Baldwin, Sophie, Elizabeth Holroyd, and Roger Burrows. Forthcoming. "Luxified Troglodytism? Mapping the Subterranean Geographies of Plutocratic London." *arq: Architectural Research Quarterly.*

Batty, David, Caelainn Barr, and Pamela Duncan. 2018. "What Lies Beneath: The Subterranean Secrets of the Super-Rich." *Guardian*, May 7. www.theguardian.com/money/2018/may/07 /going-underground-the-subterranean-secrets -of-londons-super-rich.

BBC. 2015. *Millionaire Basement Wars*. YouTube video, 1:21:07. Posted May 28. www.youtube.com /watch?v=sLJ0zZQb9x0.

BBC4. 2013. *The Secret History of Our Streets*. YouTube video, 59:36. Posted February 24, 2014. youtube .com/watch?v=yyUhMlEZh0I.

Beaverstock, Jonathan, and Iain Hay. 2016. "They've 'Never Had It So Good': The Rise and Rise of the Super-Rich and Wealth Inequality." In Hay and Beaverstock 2016: 1–17.

Beaverstock, Jonathan, Philip Hubbard, and John Rennie Short. 2004. "Getting Away with It? Exposing the Geographies of the Super-Rich." *Geoforum* 35, no. 4: 401–7.

Budd, Lucy. 2016. "Flights of Indulgence (or How the Very Wealthy Fly): The Aeromobile Patterns and Practices of the Super Rich." In Hay and Beaverstock 2016: 302–21.

Burrows, Roger, Richard Webber, and Rowland Atkinson. 2016. "Welcome to 'Pikettyville'? Mapping London's Alpha Territories." *Sociological Review* 65, no. 2: 184–201.

Butler, Tim. 2007. "For Gentrification?" *Environment and Planning A* 39, no. 1: 162–81.

Butler, Tim, and Loretta Lees. 2006. "Super-Gentrification in Barnsbury, London: Globalization and Gentrifying Global Elites at the Neighbourhood Level." *Transactions of the Institute of British Geographers* 31, no. 4: 467–87.

Capgemini. 2018. *World Wealth Report 2017.* www.worldwealthreport.com.

Clark, Eric. 2005. "The Order and Simplicity of Gentrification—A Political Challenge." In *Gentrification in a Global Context: The New Urban Colonialism?*, edited by Rowland Atkinson and Gary Bridge, 256–64. London: Routledge.

Cunningham, Niall. 2017. "Making and Mapping Britain's 'New Ordinary Elite.'" *Urban Geography.* Published online ahead of print, October 26. doi.org/10.1080/02723638.2017.1390721.

Davison, Gethin, Kim Dovey, and Ian Woodcock. 2012. "'Keeping Dalston Different': Defending Place-Identity in East London." *Planning Theory and Practice* 13, no. 1: 47–69.

DeVerteuil, Geoffrey, and David Manley. 2017. "Overseas Investment into London: Imprint, Impact, and Pied-à-terre Urbanism." *Environment and Planning A* 49, no. 6: 1308–23.

Elliott, Larry. 2018. "Inequality Gap Widens as Forty-Two People Hold Same Wealth as 3.7bn Poorest." *Guardian*, January 21. www.theguardian.com/inequality/2018/jan/22/inequality-gap-widens-as-42-people-hold-same-wealth-as-37bn-poorest.

Fernandez, Rodrigo, Annelore Hofman, and Manuel Aalbers. 2016. "London and New York as a Safe Deposit Box for the Transnational Wealth Elite." *Environment and Planning A* 48, no. 12: 2443–61.

Forrest, Ray, Bart Wissink, and Sin Yee Koh, eds. 2017. *Cities and the Super-Rich: Real Estate, Elite Practices, and Urban Political Economies.* London: Palgrave.

Glass, Ruth. 1964. "Aspects of Change." In *London: Aspects of Change*, edited by Ruth Glass, Eric Hobsbawm, Henry Pollins, et al., xii–xlii. London: Macgibbon and Kee.

Glucksberg, Luna. 2016. "A View from the Top." *City* 20, no. 2: 238–55.

Graham, Stephen. 2015. "Luxified Skies: How Vertical Urban Housing Became an Elite Preserve." *City* 19, no. 5: 618–45.

Hay, Iain, ed. 2013. *Geographies of the Super-Rich.* Cheltenham, UK: Edward Elgar.

Hay, Iain, and Jonathan Beaverstock, eds. 2016. *Handbook on Wealth and the Super-Rich.* Cheltenham, UK: Edward Elgar

Jackson, Emma, and Michaela Benson. 2014. "Neither 'Deepest, Darkest Peckham' nor 'Run-of-the-Mill' East Dulwich: The Middle Classes and Their 'Others' in an Inner-London Neighbourhood." *International Journal of Urban and Regional Research* 38, no. 4: 1195–1210.

Lees, Loretta. 2003. "Super-Gentrification: The Case of Brooklyn Heights, New York City." *Urban Studies* 40, no. 12: 2487–2509.

Lees, Loretta, and Hyun Bang Shin, eds. 2015. *Global Gentrifications: Uneven Development and Displacement.* Bristol, UK: Policy.

Lees, Loretta, Hyuan Bang Shin, and Ernesto Lopez-Morales. 2016. *Planetary Gentrification.* Bristol, UK: Polity.

Lees, Loretta, Tom Slater, and Elvin Wyly, eds. 2010. *The Gentrification Reader.* London: Routledge.

Lees, Loretta, Tom Slater, and Elvin Wyly. 2013. *Gentrification.* London: Routledge.

McCarthy, John, and Ross Kilgour. 2011. "Planning for Subterranean Residential Development in the UK." *Planning Practice and Research* 26, no. 1: 71–94.

Minton, Anna. 2017. *Big Capital: Who Is London For?* London: Penguin.

Oxfam International. 2010. *An Economy for the Ninety-Nine Percent.* www.oxfam.org/en/research/economy-99.

Oxfam International. 2016. *An Economy for the One Percent: How Privilege and Power in the Economy Drive Extreme Inequality and How This Can Be Stopped.* oxf.am/Znhx.

Pahl, Ray. 1975. *Whose City? And Further Essays on Urban Society.* Harmondsworth, UK: Penguin.

Piketty, Thomas. 2014. *Capital in the Twenty-First Century.* Cambridge, MA: Harvard University Press

Seife, Charles. 2014. "'The Billionaires' Space Club." *Slate,* December 30. www.slate.com/articles/health_and_science/space_20/2014/12/billionaires_private_space_rocket_ships_elon_musk_and_richard_branson_go.html.

Spence, Emma. 2017. "Beyond the City: Exploring the Maritime Geographies of the Super-Rich." In Forrest, Wissink, and Koh 2017: 107–26.

Steinberg, Phillip, Elizabeth Nyman, and Mauro Caraccioli. 2012. "Atlas Swam: Freedom, Capital, and Floating Sovereignties in the Seasteading Vision." *Antipode* 44, no. 4: 1532–50.

Streeck, William. 2016. *How Will Capitalism End? Essays on a Failing System.* London: Penguin.

Sunday Times Magazine. 2018. "Rich List 2017." May 13.

Urry, John. 2013. "The Super-Rich and Offshore Worlds." In *Elite Mobilities,* edited by Thomas Birtchnell and Javier Caletrío, 226–40. London: Routledge.

Walker, Annabel, and Peter Jackson. 1987. *Kensington and Chelsea: A Social and Architectural History.* London: John Murray.

Webber, Richard, and Roger Burrows. 2016. "Life in an Alpha Territory: Discontinuity and Conflict in an Elite London 'Village.'" *Urban Studies* 53, no. 15: 3139–54.

Webber, Richard, and Roger Burrows. 2018. *The Predictive Postcode: The Geodemographic Classification of British Society.* London: Sage.

Weeden, Kim, and David Grusky. 2012. "The Three Worlds of Inequality." *American Journal of Sociology* 117, no. 6: 1723–85.

Wilkins, Kathryn. 2013. "A Study of the Dominance of the Super-Wealthy in London's West End during the Nineteenth Century." In Hay 2013: 110–22.

Roger Burrows is professor of cities at Newcastle University. His most recent book (coauthored with Richard Webber) is *The Predictive Postcode: The Geodemographic Classification of British Society* (2018).

Caroline Knowles is professor of sociology at Goldsmiths, University of London, and the director of the British Academy's Cities and Infrastructure Programme. Her most recent book is *Flip-Flop: A Journey through Globalisation's Backroads* (2014).

TOP CEOs, FINANCIALIZATION, and the CREATION of the SUPER-RICH ECONOMY

Aeron Davis

Abstract This piece takes a close look at top CEOs in the United Kingdom. CEOs are not only among the ranks of today's super-rich, they have played a vital part in the evolution of an economic system that supports the super-rich generally. As the article argues, they have done this in two key ways: first, by promoting to news media and policy makers a set of financialized free-market ideas about managing the economy, and second, by managing large companies as financial assets for the benefit of financiers and the super-rich. In both ways, they have encouraged financialization and the funneling of capital away from the real economy and ordinary employees, and upward toward the super-rich. The article is based on thirty interviews with top UK business leaders, including twenty Financial Times Stock Exchange 100 CEOs, as well as other demographic and qualitative data.

Keywords financialization, elites, corporations, financial markets, CEOs

This article looks at large company CEOs in the United Kingdom. Not only are such "captains of industry" members of the super-rich, but they have played a vital role in the creation of the economic system that supports the super-rich. They have done this in two ways: by publicly and privately promoting neoliberal market philosophies that facilitate financialization and extreme inequality, and by managing major corporations as financial assets and investment vehicles for wealthy investors rather than for the benefit of the wider economy. As such, they have been key architects of a system

Cultural Politics, Volume 15, Issue 1, © 2019 Duke University Press
DOI: 10.1215/17432197-7289542

that increasingly sucks capital out of the real economy, away from ordinary citizens, to then syphon it off to financial institutions and the super-rich.

In many ways, big company bosses are the public face of the super-rich. After several decades of neoliberal economic policy making, we appear to be entering a new gilded age of corporate behemoths, billionaire businessmen, and extreme inequality. Then as now, vast personal fortunes were built on the back of industrial monopolies. Then, it was the likes of Andrew Carnegie, John D. Rockefeller, Andrew Mellon, J. P. Morgan, and Cornelius Vanderbilt. Now, it is Jeff Bezos, Mark Zuckerberg, Bill Gates, Carlos Slim, and Amancio Ortega. Such business leaders are seen as drivers of the capitalist economy in all its historical manifestations. Corporate CEOs have created such economies while also profiting hugely from them.

However, in today's gilded age the economic system, and therefore the basis of extreme wealth and inequality, is different. Instead of big industrial companies producing energy, commodities, and transport, an increasing proportion of corporations and billionaires profit from not making anything. It is financiers, investors, rentiers, and the new owners of digital platforms who are profiting most (financiers also did well in the first gilded age). Financialized (Krippner 2011) and "platform" (Srnicek 2017) forms of capitalism sit at the heart of modern economies and growing income inequality. Such systems are far more detached from the real economy of goods, physical infrastructure, and employees. They are less nation bound and more global and mobile. States and real economies depend on them, but they have less dependence on states and real economies. In fact, they provide the kinds of extensive, global infrastructures and

networks needed for extracting national capital, funneling it toward and then securing it for the global super-rich.

Although CEOs play a vital, creative role in developing and managing the new super-rich economy, relatively few end up joining their ranks through their managerial salaries alone. Most of those that do, do so through other means (inheritance, shares, financial investments, property). The majority, although highly rewarded, do more to enrich others: a variety of financial elites, oligarchs, corrupt politicians, and property magnates. In fact, key corporate figures, including many with high public profiles, increasingly appear to be subservient agents of big finance and the super-rich.

This article explores the contribution of top CEOs to this billionaire-generating system. While there is quite a lot written on this topic, much of it is based on quantitative data on capital shifts or company reports. There remains relatively little in the way of more close-up, qualitative academic studies of CEOs, which seek to explain these developments at a more micro level. This article attempts to fill in some of this gap with a focused social and cultural investigation of UK Financial Times Stock Exchange (FTSE 100) CEOs. It draws on three forms of evidence. The first is a set of thirty semistructured interviews with top CEOs: twenty from FTSE 100 companies and, for comparison, ten selected from a list of the top one hundred private companies. The second is a demographic audit of all FTSE 100 CEOs in 2014, drawing on multiple sources. The third is an analysis of trends revealed by existing surveys of British CEOs going back to the 1970s.

The article is in four parts. The first discusses key mechanisms of the UK economy that support the super-rich, situating FTSE 100 CEOs within that system. It argues that the generation of extreme wealth and inequality is more a result of financialization than neoliberalism. Corporate heads have come to play an important intermediary and facilitating role in the financialized economy. The second part looks at the ways CEOs have done this, focusing on their personal promotion of financialized capitalism. On the one hand, they are the public face of the economy, the "primary definers" (Hall et al. 1978) of wealth creation in the media. On the other, they influence government policy making as they alternate between financial and political networks, providing vital connectivity between the two.

The third part looks at the reshaping of CEOs themselves by tracing how their professional profiles have changed with the advance of financialized capitalism. This reveals that, over recent decades, those who have risen to the top are those most equipped to direct companies toward serving "shareholder value." This new generation of CEOs are more likely to be drawn from finance and accounting, and they also now operate according to an expectation of shorter leadership tenures. So, they are more able and more incentivized to achieve quick profits for wealthy investors with limited investment horizons. The fourth part documents some of the key business strategies adopted by such FTSE CEOs, arguing that they are increasingly geared toward advancing share price increases rather than long-term company innovation, employment, and stable growth. In effect, they have come to manage large corporations as if they were merely the financial assets and investment vehicles of super-rich investors.

CEOs and the Super-Rich Economy

Historically and now, large company CEOs have been closely associated with the super-rich. They are both very wealthy and key participants in capitalist democracies in all their manifestations. In classic and post-Marxist accounts, those owners and managers of the means of production have worked closely with the state to maintain wealth and control. In critical elite studies (Mills 1956; Domhoff [1967] 2014; Useem 1984; Scott 1979), corporate elites and business leaders shared power with other elite sectors to ensure their hegemony in the United States and United Kingdom.

It is also widely assumed that corporations and their CEOs have played a lead role in the rise of neoliberalism since the late 1970s (Crouch 2004, 2011; Harvey 2007; Mirowski and Plehwe 2009). Neoliberalism has several elements (see Larner 2000). It is a political project and policy framework derived from a broader set of ideas and values oriented around individual freedoms and choices. It is also an economic paradigm linked to neoclassical economics, which emphasizes market mechanisms over state ones for social and economic management. In practice, it has directed a set of political and economic policies across the world, which are closely associated with growing inequality (see Chang 2010; Wilkinson and Pickett 2010; Piketty 2014). These include supply-side measures such as low taxes and less regulation, monetarist policy levers over fiscal ones, programs of privatization and market deregulation, reduced employee and union rights, scaled-down welfare state provision, globalization, and open trading borders.

Although neoliberalism has been applied quite differently and to different degrees across the globe (see Fourcade 2009), inequality has continued to grow everywhere (Piketty 2014). In fact, historical data show that the Gini coefficient, an inequality measure that had been declining steadily in the postwar period, went into reverse in the United States and United Kingdom at the end of the 1970s. This was precisely the time that the neoliberal policy era began implementation under the Reagan and Thatcher regimes. Despite a number of economic crises, inequality and the ranks of the super-rich have continued to increase ever since (see Hardoon 2017; UBS-PwC 2017).

Clearly, big business and big business leaders have benefited from programs associated with the neoliberal turn, including privatization, deregulation, the erosion of trade union rights, and reduced rates of taxation for both corporations and high income earners (see Crouch 2011; Freeland 2012; Wedel 2014). Average CEOs have done extremely well financially over this period. In 1979, mean US CEO pay was thirty-eight times that of the average worker. By 2005 it was 262 times (Palley 2007: 14). In the UK, in 1998, FTSE 100 CEO pay was forty-seven times that of the average employee. By 2012 it had reached 185 times average (High Pay Commission 2012). Take a look at any list of the ultra-wealthy, in the *Sunday Times Rich List* or *Forbes's World's Billionaires List*, and corporate heads feature prominently.

However, the focus of many critical scholars on neoliberalism has distracted from another key economic transformation: financialization. Financialization and neoliberalism are clearly related and are frequently discussed as either mutually reinforcing or having a direct causal link (e.g., Duménil and Lévy 2004; Epstein 2005; Lazzarato 2009; Fine 2012). However, financialization has many distinct elements (see Davis and Walsh 2017). Most importantly for this discussion, several such elements have proved essential for the rapid growth of the super-rich class. Arguably, it is financialization rather than

neoliberalism that has done most to create extreme inequalities and the rising number of global billionaires.

Financialization, in Thomas Palley's words (2007: 2), "is a process whereby financial markets, financial institutions, and financial elites gain greater influence over economic policy and economic outcomes. Financialization transforms the functioning of economic systems at both the macro and micro levels." At the start of this century it was becoming clear that a process of financialization had been taking place in conjunction with the spread of neoliberal-driven free-market economics (see Engelen 2008). Several overviews (Epstein 2005; Palley 2007, 2013; Stockhammer 2010; Krippner 2011) recorded how this transformation has taken place in the United States, United Kingdom, and elsewhere, tracing patterns of capital accumulation as they shifted toward the financial sector.

Most obviously, financial market activities and values have grown hugely relative to both the state and the real, productive economy of goods and services. Thus the capital managed by banks, as well as their ability to create credit, has risen several fold compared to state expenditures, the capital of central banks, or national gross domestic products (GDPs). The United Kingdom is one of the countries where the shift has been particularly pronounced in recent decades. Until the 1970s, UK bank assets had been equal to roughly half the value of UK GDP for a century. By the mid-2000s, they had risen to five times the value of GDP (Haldane 2010). In 1979, the equity value of the stock market was roughly two-fifths of government income. By 2012 it was worth three times government income (see Davis and Walsh 2017). According to John Kay (2016), currently some 97 percent of "money" in the UK economy is just circulating around the financial sector. Only 3 percent is either fiat (paper) money or capital lent to firms and individuals operating in the material economy.

In effect, processes and institutions associated with financialization are geared toward extracting capital out of the real economy and from ordinary people, then passing it to be managed and invested by financial institutions and the super-rich. Banking becomes less about capital investment in nonfinancial companies, or ordinary savings and loans. Instead, it is more about short-term profit seeking through activity within financial, property, and other markets. Large NFCs (nonfinancial corporations) are increasingly run to create "shareholder value" by any means, including through purely financial activities (see Crotty 2005; Froud et al. 2006). Financialized economies actively enroll citizens into finance (see Seabrooke 2006; Leyshon and Thrift 2007; Lazzarato 2012) through a mixture of personal credit card and mortgage debt, investment of public pension funds, and securitization. Financial intermediaries then enable rentier behavior and global tax avoidance and evasion on behalf of the global super-rich (Epstein and Jayadev 2005; Shaxon 2011; Piketty 2014).

However, although many large company CEOs have been made wealthy through financialization, others have benefited more. Yes, there are many super-rich business leaders with high profiles. However, there are many more billionaires who have inherited their wealth or gained it through political corruption, financial investment, or rentier activities. CEOs may earn millions and be the object of tabloid outrage for their incomes, but top financiers and super-rich investors earn tens or hundreds of millions annually. Of the twenty best-paid FTSE 100 bosses in 2017

(*Business Insider* 2017), only two made it onto the *Sunday Times Rich List* (2017): Martin Sorrell, the highest paid, came 258th, and Simon Borrows came 484th. As recent accounts of elites note (Savage and Williams 2008; Freeland 2012; Davis and Williams 2017), it is the financial sector that has provided the fastest contribution to the growing ranks of the global 1 percent (or 0.001 percent) and has boosted the expanding rentier class (Duménil and Lévy 2004; Piketty 2014).

At the same time, traditional CEOs have fallen down the elite pecking order in various ways (see Moran 2008; Mizruchi 2013; Naim 2013; Davis and Williams 2017; Davis 2018). They have become more fragmented and less collective, and their levels of influence in Washington and Westminster have declined. There is a clear sense that the dominant CEOs of the recent past now have far less political power and economic authority than they once did. Top financiers, a select group of tech industry leaders, and the super-rich have taken their place.

This leaves us asking, what exactly is happening at the social and organizational levels? How have CEOs as individuals shifted their professional behaviors and practices in ways that, almost imperceptibly, have aided the expansion of big finance and boosted the ranks and incomes of the super-rich? The question has added bite because it also needs to explain how corporate CEOs have colluded in a process that has rewarded and given more power and influence to others.

This is the question addressed in the following investigation of UK FTSE 100 CEOs. Most of the largest UK-based companies are listed on the London Stock Exchange. In the financialization literature, it is these companies, as opposed to those owned by individuals or funded by conventional banks, that have been most systematically affected by the demands of the global financial system.

The research drew on three main forms of qualitative data on the UK business elite in 2014. The first was a series of semistructured interviews with thirty large company heads: twenty public FTSE 100 CEOs and, for comparison, ten CEOs of private *Sunday Times* Top Track 100 Companies, as ranked by sales. Each group was selected as a purposive sample, reflective of the distribution of industry sectors in the index (e.g., manufacturing, finance, construction, retail).[1] Interviewees were asked about a number of themes, including their background and education, social relations and professional networks, information sources and decision-making processes, larger business strategies, and wider views on and relations with nonbusiness sectors (government, the financial sector, media, unions, and communities). Interview lengths varied, with most being forty-five minutes to an hour. In total, they generated over 250,000 words of transcript material. This was then coded and aggregated. Interviewees are named unless anonymity was requested. The sample of thirty is relatively small, although it is also an extremely difficult group to gain access to with a limited pool of potential subjects. At the same time, with such a small number, the data are less likely to be representative and more likely to contain instances of bias. Thus the findings have limitations while also providing some directions for further research.

The second form of data consisted of an audit of demographic and biographical information on all FTSE 100 CEOs in their posts in mid-2014. Sources were mainly individual profiles from *Who's Who*, *World of CEOs*, *Bloomberg*, and *Business Week*. Information collected included school

education, higher education, postgraduate qualifications, nationality, and tenure of CEO position. The third form of data was a collection of past social studies and surveys of CEOs going back to the early 1970s.

FTSE 100 CEOs as Promoters of Financialized Capitalism

First, there is quite a bit of evidence to show that large UK company CEOs support neoliberal policy agendas in general, and the Conservative Party more specifically (Fidler 1981; Hill 1990; Boswell and Peters 1997; Davis 2002, 2017). Periodic surveys show they have united around an antistate, promarket ideology, promoting privatization, competition, deregulation, lower taxes, reduced union and labor rights, globalization, and free trade. In election data going back to the 1980s, the percentage of "captains of industry" voting Conservative has been over 85 percent, with the exception of 1997 when it was 69 percent (Davis 2017: 239).

The interview cohort, both public and private, appeared to reflect this pattern accurately. Twenty-seven of the thirty made two or more statements of a promarket, antistate nature. In terms of party allegiances, four-fifths were Conservative Party supporters. This came out in a mixture of public statements and direct interview responses. The alignment of the remaining fifth was not clear.

FTSE 100 CEOs have been vociferous promoters, not always consciously, of financialized forms of neoliberalism. While publicly and privately supporting free markets and reduced states, they have also supported and/or colluded in a series of economic policy shifts that have aided financialization's growth. By pushing market deregulation, new accounting practices, globalization, and free trade generally, they have spurred on financial engineering, capital concentrations, and global liquidity, all vital to financialization's rise. Their cooperation with political and financial elites on a number of changes in corporate governance, privatization methods, takeover regimes, and fiscal practices have handed more wealth and influence over to big finance and the super-rich (Davis and Walsh 2016).

FTSE 100 CEO support for the neoliberal policy agenda has come in several forms: via public promotion of financialized, free-market economic policies in mainstream media; through funding of and direct access to the Conservative Party; and by forming a vital bridging network between financial and state elites.

Public promotion of financialized free-market policy has come through business and financial media. Studies of news content in the 1970s and 1980s (Hall et al. 1978; Glasgow University Media Group 1980) found that business leaders and government sources dominated coverage of economic affairs in mainstream news. They acted as the primary definers, framing public debates about industrial action and economic policy. Business voices, especially those of CEOs and City-based analysts, came to dominate all the more from the 1990s onward as the public relations and investor relations industries expanded (Parsons 1989; Davis 2002). Since the 2007–8 crash, CEOs have continued to use their primary definer status in economic and business news to support welfare state cuts, reduce corporate taxes, and weaken new business and financial regulations. They have also blamed government and the Labour Party, rather than financiers, for the economic crisis (Davis 2011; Knowles 2015; Berry 2016). Their support for such policies and austerity economics was evident during

the 2015 and 2017 elections, encouraging a public perception that the Conservatives were far more economically competent than Labour.

Second, as Michael Moran (2008) points out, business leaders have maintained direct forms of personal political influence through the Conservative Party, even as other forms of collective business influence have declined (Daguerre 2014). Studies of parliamentary candidates and MPs consistently show that people from business and finance make up by far the largest proportion of the Conservative Party (Norris and Lovenduski 1997; Childs, Lovenduski, and Campbell 2005). Wealthy business and financial donors also contribute the great majority of party funds. Business lobbyists continue to gain greater access to ministers and civil servants than other sector interests (Mitchell 1997; Miller and Dinan 2008; Wilks-Heeg, Blick, and Crone 2012).

Third, what became increasingly apparent during the interviews was the high level of networking and meetings that FTSE 100 CEOs had with both financial and political elites, especially when compared with the private company CEO cohort. Private company CEOs were far less London based, spoke little about such networks, and were rather less likely to have regular dealings with civil servants, ministers, and big investors. In contrast, most FTSE companies have either their head offices in London or large permanent bases there. Most FTSE CEOs were self-confessed "networkers," devoting a large part of their time to meeting leaders at different levels of government, business, and finance. In effect, FTSE CEOs were very much part of metropolitan-based, national, and international networks of corporate and noncorporate elites:

Stephen Hester: I've always been in international businesses that deal with lots of other businesses, and deal with government and so on and so forth. . . . It's reinforced, because, well, there's pure work and then there's what I call social work, which is cocktail parties and CBI meetings and international conferences and so on, where you meet people in a sort of quasi-social setting.

FTSE 100 chiefs regularly moved between big investors and government policy makers and regulators. As they alternated between the City (the financial sector) and Westminster (the political sector), they established a sense of network connectivity between the two. So, on the one hand, they talked of needing to meet major shareholders to agree on corporate investment, strategy, and financial goals:

Paul Walsh: But ultimately the final judge of whether it's the right thing to do is the shareholders.

Ian Cheshire: But above all else just tell the owners of the business [investors] what you're doing and why.

On the other hand, they came into frequent contact with ministers, civil servants, and others in government. This would be for a variety of reasons: direct lobbying, negotiations with regulators, social invitations, and being volunteers for government-organized task forces or policy communities. Much of this, although regular, was informal and ad hoc, taking place instead of formal board meetings, often on the basis of CEOs advising ministers on economic policy matters:

Paul Walsh: There are so many groups that need to be paid attention to, be it governments, regulators.

Ian Cheshire: I do work for the Department of Work and Pensions. That is an extraordinary network of very senior business people who are interested in government, who meet quarterly, which Lord Brown organizes.

In effect, FTSE heads made up a key communicative network, at one end being directed by financiers, and at the other promoting free-market wisdoms to policy makers—wisdoms that also enable those CEOs to achieve their financier-agreed goals. Mairi Maclean, Charles Harvey, and Gerhardt Kling (2014), when looking at French business elites, detected a higher, more powerful and exclusive group that they referred to as "hyper-agents." These agents or "bridging" actors, they argued, were central players moving across multiple networks of elites, thus playing a key role in maintaining the French establishment status quo. Arguably, FTSE 100 CEOs play a similar role in UK politics and economics. They provide a fundamental level of connectivity, formal and informal, between big finance and big government. In so doing they have not only encouraged the evolution of a neoliberal, free-market policy process that has advantaged international finance, but they have reified certain financialized forms of economic management in the eyes of successive governments. Thus in the United Kingdom, as with the United States, financial markets have come to be regarded as the best institutional centers for managing the economy generally: as investors, promoters of market competition, corporate governance enforcers, and so on.

The Financialized CEO

As this next part argues, successful FTSE 100 company CEOs have also adapted to financialization in terms of their professional identity and function. They have become less diverse in their educational backgrounds. In particular, there has been a clear growth in those who have studied accounting and/or taken the finance route to the top. They have also come to operate under an assumption that they are likely to be in a post for a relatively short period. Thus, they have been reconditioned to achieve results within two- to three-year accounting cycles.

In general, there has been a longer trend toward professionalizing the CEO occupation. Going back four decades, CEOs had a greater variety of educational backgrounds, coming from science, engineering, the social sciences, and professions such as law. In 1974, only 7 percent had some kind of business degree. In Mairi Maclean, Charles Harvey, and John Press's study (2006) using 1998 data, the trends showed that roughly a third of CEOs had a business-related degree, a third a science one, and a third had something from the arts, social sciences, or professions. Moving to the present, the 2014 audit of FTSE 100 CEOs shows that 48 percent have a first degree in business studies, economics, or a related subject. Sciences and engineering have dropped a bit, and all other subjects now make up only 15 percent of degrees. In effect, creative and critical higher education subjects have been minimized among today's business leadership.

Most significant has been the rise of financial over all other forms of expertise among top CEOs. In John Fidler's (1981: 102) study, using 1974 data, 18 percent gained an accounting qualification, and just 10 percent had taken the finance route to the top. Maclean, Harvey, and Press (2006: 131), using 1998 data, found that 27 percent had come up through the finance and accounting pathway. In my 2014

demographic audit, many of those with professional, business-oriented degrees included curriculum elements of finance or accounting. Twenty-six percent had a higher education accounting degree or other qualification, with 12 percent having worked at one of the big four international accounting firms. Fifty percent of CEOs had held at least one senior financial position (e.g., finance director, CFO) during their career pathway prior to becoming a CEO. Fifty-three percent in total had accounting and/or finance included in their professional qualifications and/or pathways.

The interview cohort of thirty matched this pattern, considerably more so for the FTSE 100 respondents than the private company cohort. Seventeen of the twenty FTSE 100 chiefs had economics, accounting, or related degrees and/or an MBA. For those listed company CEOs, the accounting and finance route was clearly a common pathway to follow:

David Nish: Chartered accountancy training to me I think is really one of the best professions to go into, because of the opportunity you do get to access business. You know, and in some ways, particularly through initially the auditing route, you actually get to access business at a reasonably high level quite quickly.

Second, what became clear during the research was just how much CEO tenures had declined in such large international corporations. Chrystia Freeland (2012: 53) noted that the average tenure of a Fortune 500 CEO had fallen from 9.5 years to 3.5 over a decade. Several interviewees commented on this, and the 2014 audit confirmed it. A third of FTSE 100 CEOs had been in their posts less than two years, and another third less than five years. Private company heads, in contrast, seemed to have been in post for twice as long on average. The longest-serving public limited company (PLC) heads were usually those who had started the business themselves, like Martin Sorrell or Ian Wood. This sense of short-term existence was clear to those who were interviewed, especially in relation to justifying their huge pay levels and bonus systems:

Martin Sorrell: One of the problems is that CEOs last on average at the moment less than five years and if you're a CMO [chief management officer] in America you might last two years.

This has consequences for FTSE 100 CEO behaviors. Indeed, the interviews revealed a clear sense of the pressures felt to achieve short-term profits and share price increases in limited time spans. CEOs in general, private or public, talked about balancing long-term and short-term goals, but private heads all strongly emphasized the importance of the long-term. Most said they made only "long-term decisions," promoted the "steady, continuous building up" of a company by, for example, developing settled teams, investing in employee training and research. In contrast, many PLC heads talked about the impatience and "blind short-termism" of big shareholders, and the pressures to pay dividends or "gear up" (use debt finance to purchase assets):

Warren East: The fund manager is completely motivated by delivering the best possible return for this year, and if the companies which deliver that best possible return this year aren't around next year, that doesn't matter. . . . It means that there is pressure to do sort of short-term things which, from a business point of view, are not

sustainable. . . . I've had investors request a one-on-one meeting with the CEO and sit me down and say: "You should be leveraging up the balance sheet and taking on lots of debt."

Such answers confirmed the findings of other studies that argue that London Stock Exchange quoted companies have become overly focused on short-term share movements (Froud et al. 2006; Kay 2012; Cox 2013). Since funds hold shares for ever shorter periods, this is no surprise. The average length of time by which a share is held has dropped from eight years in the 1960s to just three months this decade (High Pay Commission 2012). Another study of FTSE 100 annual report statements on CEO performance and pay (High Pay Commission 2013) found that ninety-six of them used either EPS (earnings per share), TSR (total shareholder returns), or both as key performance measures. Only thirty-eight used "alternative" nonfinancial measures such as employment retention or customer satisfaction or innovation in their performance metrics, and only seven contained LTIPs (long-term incentive plans).

What was concerning in the interviews was that several respondents were simultaneously aware of these short-term pressures while also admitting that figures could be simply manipulated over a two- to three-year period:

Anonymous FTSE 100 CEO: When people only focus short term then they start hiding stuff as well. Give me a balance sheet or short-term incentives, short term sales . . . I'll change it for your assumptions, I'll get you a twelve-month result, a piece of cake. It's going to burn me next year, or maybe in two years' time or as long as three, but any idiot can get a short-term result.

This combination of short-termism, ability to manipulate accounts, and the expectation that one's tenure was unlikely to be long, had obvious implications for CEOs. The clear message was that corporate heads were personally incentivized to maximize short-term performance on behalf of big investors, regardless of the long-term consequences for the company or employees. As one interviewee put it:

Samir Brikho: You read about the average CEO and the businesses is like almost becoming three years. And if that's the case, it's bad news for the industry. . . . If you don't spend it on the R and D then you can convert that to profit. That's great if you are there only two or three years but do you kill the company maybe later on. . . . So, if I'd been optimizing only for the first two years in order to make the big buck at the third year and then thank you very much and bye, that would not be great for the company's future.

Financialized Management Strategies and Decision Making

How do CEOs manage their companies to achieve big investor demand for short-term share price rises? All interviewees, private and public, were asked about their larger business strategies and the processes they used for making major decisions. The discussions revealed several approaches. These fell into two categories. The first involved directing regular mergers, acquisitions, asset sales, and other activities that were designed to keep up shareholder interest and company share values. The second guided companies away from risky innovations and long-term investments, instead orienting them toward maximizing low-risk profits. In effect, FTSE 100 CEOs had adopted a series of strategies designed to manage financier

and super-rich capital investments to gain short-term returns without taking on longer-term risks and liabilities.

The first strategy involves maintaining what Peter Folkman et al. (2007) term an "economy of permanent restructuring." As they and others have noted (Froud et al. 2006; Kay 2012; Cox 2013), successful publicly listed company CEOs continually enter into big change activities and financial deal making. Activities include using debt finance and leverage, merger and acquisition activity, asset sell-offs, equity buy-backs, and global tax avoidance.

Several FTSE 100 heads interviewed, especially those who had held their position for more than a few years, appeared to conform to such patterns. They had long track records of doing big deals and large-scale restructuring. Half had done multiple mergers and acquisitions, and two-thirds had made major disposals. Such activity grows and reshapes a company in quick, large steps rather than expanding it steadily and organically. It is the kind of activity that maintains investor interest, boosts share prices, and brings profits to a range of financial intermediaries and institutional shareholders. This is despite the fact that most studies of takeovers find the large majority do not add value in the long term to a company (Sudarsanam 1995; Hutton 1996; Bootle 2009). For some CEOs, all this activity was clearly connected to their success and longevity in post:

Gareth Davis: The Harvard Business Review quoted me as being the thirty-third most successful CEO of all-time, recently, in terms of value creation for shareholders . . . obviously people say you made a lot of money for the institutions. . . . We did two mega deals. There was one in 2002 and one in 2008. I mean they were multibillion deals with associated rights issues and everything. But I think we did twenty-six in all.

Accordingly, the London Stock Exchange is now regarded as one of the top exchanges to float new companies and carry out demerger and merger activity. Since the 1980s the United Kingdom has had a significantly higher level of takeover activity than other advanced economies (Jackson and Miyajima 2007). From 1998 to 2005, takeover activity as a percentage of GDP was 21.8 percent, double that of the United States where it was 10.7 percent. The United Kingdom also had the highest success rate for hostile takeovers at 67 percent (Jackson and Miyajima 2007). Several CEOs commented on the general pressure from investment banks and large investors to get involved in such activities in the London Stock Exchange:

Anonymous FTSE 100 CEO: There is so much pressure to do deals in London, more than anywhere else in the world. The banks, the brokers, the PRs, they all make money from these deals. The UK is unique. I never did these deals unless I was convinced it would help me and I did do some 100 deals at ——. If you don't deal you get a reputation for being "dull." . . . The long-term economy will not have [benefited]. It's only the shareholders and the institutional intermediaries that would.

The second general strategy involved guiding the company away from higher risk practices of innovation and long-term investment. Instead, FTSE CEOs preferred to exploit their size and position, existing products and customer bases, and to seek out monopoly opportunities. Such approaches, once again, are inherently short term in nature and are geared to

gaining greater returns on capital rather than developing anything new or long term.

This first became clear when comparing attitudes toward "risk" during decision making between PLC and private company CEOs. Both sets were cognizant of risk. However, private CEOs talked in terms of needing to take "measured risks," with several advocating sensible risk taking as being necessary for innovation in business. PLC heads, on the other hand, talked a lot about risk but did so far more in defensive terms. They talked about needing to make risk "evaluations" or "audits" before making big decisions, and the need to implement risk reduction strategies. The term *risk* was rarely mentioned by private company CEOs but over one hundred times in the twenty interviews with FTSE 100 bosses.

This sense of risk in making decisions seemed to feed directly into larger company strategies. Private heads thought about long-term plans and investment. They looked to a range of sources for new business inspiration, from news and popular culture to businesses in very different sectors. In contrast, FTSE 100 heads tended to be more managerial than entrepreneurial, more influenced by business consultancy literature, and more insular. When asked about their sources of inspiration, it was clear they spent a lot of time observing and talking to other business leaders in their own sector. Rather like financial investors whose trading decisions are based on what other traders are doing (Keynes 1936), PLC chiefs keep a close eye on their competition.

A third, when asked about strategy and innovation, said they much preferred to "steal ideas" or be a "fast follower" rather than an innovator. As they explained, new ideas were hard to come by, true innovation was risky, and the window of exclusivity was now much shorter as rivals copied you. Such a finding tallies with one UK study (Ownership Commission 2012: 35) which found that 75 percent of managers would avoid investing in projects with potential long-term value creation if they were damaging to short-term earnings. As one interviewee explained:

Alan Parker: We went through a big investment in enterprise-wide systems, which frankly turned out to be not best in class for our various activities. And I would say from that experience . . . I would definitely always want to see it working elsewhere. Rather than paying the price of being a leading-edge innovator, I'd much rather be a fast follower.

What also came through was a sense of exploiting existing resources, advantages, and market dominant positions. So, a very common business strategy involved better utilizing of existing resources, products, and customers. Thus the aim was to do "the same things better," "more cheaply," or with minor variations, rather than developing risky new products. Very often, the aim was to "protect margins" or "offer more to the same customer base." Three-fifths of interviewees talked about such cautious, low-risk strategies:

Terry Leahy: The common denominator for us was actually if we keep the same customer set, can we serve that same customer set with a wider range of services as well as products? And actually, we were able to do it. . . . If you can find out something that works and keep doing it for as long as possible, then that's the way to build really big numbers, big benefits.

Two-fifths of FTSE 100 CEOs followed this logic further, stating that the best way to

gain strong profits was to gain and exploit a leading market position. This entailed moving into sectors where a company could use its size and resources to quickly become one of the dominant players. The best low-risk, high-return strategy of all was to gain a monopoly situation in a market, something a handful of CEOs openly admitted was a goal:

Guy Berruyer: Yes, if you want to be highly successful and very profitable, you might as well find a way to get sort of a micro monopoly, because that's the best way to be highly profitable. . . . Every market is highly competitive, so how do you protect your margins, how do you make sure that you make money? And there's various ways, but the best way is to create a micro monopoly.

Ultimately, most FTSE 100 CEOs followed two overall strategies (sometimes simultaneously), both of which were aimed at pleasing wealthy and institutional investors over relatively short-term horizons. One involved big eye-catching activities, such as acquisitions or asset sales, which maintained investor interest and pushed share prices up in the short term (although often not in the long term). The second involved decisions that were defensive and risk averse, and more about exploiting existing size and assets and gaining dominant market positions to increase profits. Neither involved much in the way of innovation or long-term investments. The end impression was of CEOs managing large organizations as financial assets on behalf of big investors over limited time spans.

Conclusion

FTSE 100 CEOs in the United Kingdom are clearly part of the current economic system that produces extreme wealth and inequality. They are the very public face and cheerleaders of that system. However, as this article has shown, they are more likely to be rich than super-rich. Their main function has been to facilitate financialization and the mechanisms that produce and sustain such inequalities. Although well rewarded for their part in this transition, in the process they have done more to increase the wealth and influence of others.

In some respects this makes them atypical of an emergent class of very powerful and super-rich CEOs who both manage and maintain substantial shareholdings in transnational companies. Figures such as Jeff Bezos, Mark Zuckerberg, Bernard Arnault, Amancio Ortega, and Jack Ma have merged power, wealth, and management. In other regards, FTSE UK corporate heads are typical of the larger mass of ordinarily rich managers who manage capital and assets on behalf of the super-rich class in the era of neoliberal and financialized capitalism. In Gerard Duménil and Dominique Lévy's (2018) historical overview of managerial capitalism, they remain very much intermediaries operating on behalf of the super-rich capitalist class, rather than being part of that class.

The piece then went on to explore the ways this transition has been put into effect at a more micro, sociocultural level in the UK case. Three important social mechanisms were set out to explain this. First, FTSE 100 chiefs have become lead promoters of financialized forms of free-market thinking. They have pushed their views through public media as well as through private elite networks spanning political, financial, and other super-rich elites. In effect, they have maintained vital connectivity between wealth, finance, and politics.

Second, they have adapted professionally to better service the expectations of wealthy investors and financial institutions. Thus they have become more financially expert, as a growing number have accounting qualifications and/or have worked in finance departments. That knowledge, combined with shortened CEO tenures, has worked to orient corporate behavior more toward limited, financially oriented horizons.

Third, successful business leaders have adopted strategies that do more to please big investor demands in the short term than to develop companies successfully or sustain working populations in the long term. These alternate between continual deal making to boost share prices and seeking out low-risk market opportunities, such as copying successful rivals and developing monopolies. Consequently, CEOs have moved from being key drivers and beneficiaries of neoliberalism to becoming intermediaries for financialization and servants of the super-rich.

Note

1. For FTSE 100 public limited companies (PLCs), the sectors were Finance (four interviewees), Utilities (two), Media/IT (two), Pharmaceuticals (one), Mining (two), Consumer (three), Property (two), Manufacturing (two), and Supermarkets (two). For top one hundred private companies: Retail (two), Utilities (two), Construction/Engineering (one), Wholesale/Distribution (one), Manufacturing (one), Food Production (one), Entertainment (one), and Finance (one).

Interviews

Guy Berruyer, CEO, Sage, August 29, 2014.
Samir Brikho, CEO, AMEC, April 1, 2014.
Sir Ian Cheshire, CEO, Kingfisher, January 10, 2014.
Gareth Davis, chairman, William Hill; chairman, Wolseley; chairman, D. S. Smith; former CEO and chairman, Imperial Tobacco, 1996–2010, June 27, 2013.
Warren East, former CEO, ARM, 2001–13, February 5, 2014.

Stephen Hester, CEO, Royal Bank of Scotland, November 14, 2013.

Sir Terry Leahy, former CEO, Tesco, 1997–2011, July 15, 2013.

David Nish, CEO, Standard Life, July 24, 2014.

Alan Parker, chairman, Mothercare; former CEO, Whitbread, 2004–10, July 17, 2013.

Sir Martin Sorrell, founder and CEO, WPP, September 11, 2014.

Paul Walsh, CEO, Diageo, August 28, 2013.

References

Berry, Mike. 2016. "The UK Press and the Deficit Debate." *Sociology* 50, no. 3: 542–49.

Bootle, Roger. 2009. *The Trouble with Markets: Saving Capitalism from Itself*. London: Nicholas Brealey.

Boswell, Jonathan, and James Peters. 1997. *Capitalism in Contention: Business Leaders and Political Economy in Modern Britain*. Cambridge: Cambridge University Press.

Business Insider. 2017. "The Twenty Best Paid FTSE 100 CEOs." August 3. uk.businessinsider.com /the-20-best-paid-ceos-of-the-ftse-100-2017-8.

Chang, Ha Joon. 2010. *Twenty-Three Things They Don't Tell You about Capitalism*. London: Penguin.

Childs, Sarah, Joni Lovenduski, and Rosie Campbell. 2005. *British Representation Study*. www.bbk .ac.uk/politics/our-research/archive/past -projects/british-representation-study.

Cox, George. 2013. *Cox Review: Overcoming Short-Termism within British Business: The Key to Sustained Economic Growth*. London: Labour Party.

Crotty, James. 2005. "The Neoliberal Paradox: The Impact of Destructive Product Market Competition and 'Modern' Financial Markets on Nonfinancial Corporation Performance in the Neoliberal Era." In Epstein 2005: 77–110.

Crouch, Colin. 2004. *Post-Democracy*. Cambridge: Polity.

Crouch, Colin. 2011. *The Strange Non-death of Neo-Liberalism*. Cambridge: Polity.

Daguerre, Anne. 2014. "New Corporate Elites and the Erosion of the Keynesian Social Compact." *Work, Employment, and Society* 28, no. 2: 323–34.

Davis, Aeron. 2002. *Public Relations Democracy: Public Relations, Politics, and the Mass Media in Britain*. Manchester, UK: Manchester University Press.

Davis, Aeron. 2011. "The Mediation of Finance: An Inverted Political Economy of Communication Approach." In *Media Political Economies: Hierarchies, Markets, and Finance in the Global Media Industries*, edited by Dwayne Winseck and Dal Yong Jin, 241–54. London: Bloomsbury.

Davis, Aeron. 2017. "Sustaining Corporate Class Consciousness across the New *Liquid Managerial Elite* in Britain." *British Journal of Sociology* 68, no. 2: 234–53.

Davis, Aeron. 2018. *Reckless Opportunists: Elites at the End of the Establishment*. Manchester, UK: Manchester University Press.

Davis, Aeron, and Catherine Walsh. 2016. "The Role of the State in the Financialisation of the UK Economy." *Political Studies* 64, no. 3: 666–82.

Davis, Aeron, and Catherine Walsh. 2017. "Beyond Neoliberalism: The Cultural and Epistemological Foundations of Financialization." *Theory, Culture, and Society* 34, nos. 5–6: 27–51.

Davis, Aeron, and Karel Williams. 2017. "Introduction: Elites and Power after Financialization." *Theory, Culture, and Society* 34, nos. 5–6: 3–26.

Domhoff, George. (1967) 2014. *Who Rules America?* 7th ed. Englewood Cliffs, NJ: Prentice-Hall.

Duménil, Gerard, and Dominique Lévy. 2004. *Capital Resurgent: Roots of the Neoliberal Revolution*. Translated by Derek Jeffers. Cambridge, MA: Harvard University Press.

Duménil, Gerard, and Dominique Lévy. 2018. *Managerial Capitalism: Ownership, Management, and the Coming New Mode of Production*. London: Pluto.

Engelen, Ewald. 2008. "The Case for Financialization." *Competition and Change* 12, no. 2: 111–19.

Epstein, Gerald, ed. 2005. *Financialization and the World Economy*. Cheltenham, UK: Edward Elgar.

Epstein, Gerald, and Arjun Jayadev. 2005. "The Rise of Rentier Incomes in OECD Countries: Financialization, Central Bank Policy, and Labour Solidarity." In Epstein 2005: 46–74.

Fidler, John. 1981. *The British Business Elite: Its Attitudes to Class, Status, and Power*. London: Routledge and Keagan Paul.

Fine, Ben. 2012. "Neoliberalism in Retrospect? It's Financialization Stupid." In *Developmental Politics in Transition: The Neoliberal Era and Beyond*, edited by Chang Kyung Sup, Ben Fine, and Linda Weiss, 51–69. London: Palgrave Macmillan.

Folkman, Peter, Julie Froud, Sukhdev Johal, and Karel Williams. 2007. "Working for Themselves: Financial Intermediaries and Present-Day Capitalism." *Business History* 49, no. 4: 552–72.

Fourcade, Marion. 2009. *Economists and Societies: Discipline and Profession in the United States, Britain, and France, 1890s to 1990s*. Princeton, NJ: Princeton University Press.

Freeland, Chrystia. 2012. *Plutocrats: The Rise of the New Global Super-Rich*. London: Penguin.

Froud, Julie, Sukhdev Johal, Adam Leaver, and Karel Williams. 2006. *Financialization and Strategy: Narrative and Numbers*. Abingdon, UK: Routledge.

Glasgow University Media Group. 1980. *More Bad News*. London: Routledge.

Haldane, Andrew. 2010. *The Contribution of the Financial Sector: Miracle or Mirage?* Speech at the Future of Finance Conference, London School of Economics and Political Science, July 14.

Hall, Stuart, Charles Critcher, Tony Jefferson, John Clarke, and Brian Roberts. 1978. *Policing the Crisis: Mugging, the State, and Law and Order*. London: MacMillan.

Hardoon, Deborah. 2017. *An Economy for the Ninety-Nine Percent*. Oxford: Oxfam.

Harvey, David. 2007. *A Brief History of Neoliberalism*. Oxford: Oxford University Press.

High Pay Commission. 2012. *The State of Play: One Year on from the High Pay Commission*. London: High Pay Commission.

High Pay Commission. 2013. *Paid to Perform*. London: High Pay Commission.

Hill, Stephen. 1990. "Britain: The Dominant Ideology Thesis after a Decade." In *The Dominant Ideology Thesis*, edited by Nicholas Abercrombie, Stephen Hill, and Brian Turner, 1–37. London: Unwin Hyman.

Hutton, Will. 1996. *The State We're In*. London: Vintage.

Jackson, Gregory, and Hideaki Miyajima. 2007. *Varieties of Capitalism, Varieties of Markets: Mergers and Acquisitions in Japan, Germany, France, the UK, and USA*. RIETI Discussion Paper Series 07-E-054. London: RIETI.

Kay, John. 2012. *The Key Review of UK Equity Markets and Long-Term Decision-Making*. London: Department of Business, Innovation, and Skills.

Kay, John. 2016. *Other People's Money: Masters of the Universe or Servants of the People?* London: Profile Books.

Keynes, John. 1936. *The General Theory of Employment, Interest, and Money*. London: Macmillan.

Knowles, Sophie. 2015. "Reporting the Global Financial Crisis." *Journalism Studies* 18, no. 3: 322–40.

Krippner, Gretta. 2011. *Capitalizing on Crisis: The Political Origins of the Rise of Finance*. Cambridge, MA: Harvard University Press.

Larner, Wendy. 2000. "Neoliberalism: Policy, Ideology, Governmentality." *Studies in Political Economy* 63: 5–26.

Lazzarato, Maurizio. 2009. "Neoliberalism in Action: Inequality, Insecurity, and the Reconstitution of the Social." *Theory, Culture, and Society* 26, no. 6: 109–33.

Lazzarato, Maurizio. 2012. *The Making of Indebted Man*. Cambridge, MA: MIT Press.

Leyshon, Andrew, and Nigel Thrift. 2007. "The Capitalization of Almost Everything: The Future of Finance and Capitalism." *Theory, Culture, and Society* 24, nos. 7–8: 97–115.

Maclean, Mairi, Charles Harvey, and Gerhardt Kling. 2014. "Pathways to Power: Class, Hyper-Agency, and the French Corporate Elite." *Organization Studies* 35, no. 6: 825–55.

Maclean, Mairi, Charles Harvey, and John Press. 2006. *Business Elites and Corporate Governance in France and the UK*. Basingstoke, UK: Palgrave Macmillan.

Miller, David, and Will Dinan. 2008. *A Century of Spin: How Public Relations Became the Cutting Edge of Corporate Power*. London: Pluto.

Mills, C. Wright. 1956. *The Power Elite*. Oxford: Oxford University Press.

Mirowski, Phillip, and Dieter Plehwe, eds. 2009. *The Road from Mont Pelerin: The Making of the Neoliberal Thought Collective*. Cambridge, MA: Harvard University Press.

Mitchell, Neil. 1997. *The Conspicuous Corporation: Business, Publicity, and Representative Democracy*. Ann Arbor: University of Michigan Press.

Mizruchi, Mark. 2013. *The Fracturing of the American Corporate Elite*. Cambridge, MA: Harvard University Press.

Moran, Michael. 2008. "Representing the Corporate Elite in Britain: Capitalist Solidarity and Capitalist Legitimacy." In Savage and Williams 2008: 64–79.

Naím, Moises. 2013. *The End of Power: From Boardrooms to Battlefields and Churches to States, Why Being in Charge Isn't What It Used to Be*. New York: Basic Books.

Norris, Pippa, and Joni Lovenduski. 1997. "United Kingdom." In *Passages to Power: Legislative Recruitment in Advanced Democracies*, edited by Pippa Norris, 158–86. Cambridge: Cambridge University Press.

Ownership Commission. 2012. *Plurality, Stewardship, and Engagement*. London: Ownership Commission.

Palley, Thomas. 2007. *Financialization: What It Is and Why It Matters*. Working Paper No. 525. London: Levy Economics Institute.

Palley, Thomas. 2013. *Financialization: The Economics of Finance Capital Domination*. London: Palgrave Macmillan.

Parsons, Wayne. 1989. *The Power of the Financial Press: Journalism and Economic Opinion in Britain and America*. London: Edward Elgar.

Piketty, Thomas. 2014. *Capital in the Twenty-First Century*. Cambridge, MA: Harvard University Press.

Savage, Mike, and Karel Williams, eds. 2008. *Remembering Elites*. Oxford: Wiley-Blackwell.

Scott, John. 1979. *Corporations, Classes, and Capitalism*. London: Hutchinson.

Seabrooke, Leonard. 2006. *The Social Sources of Financial Power: Domestic Legitimacy and International Financial Orders*. Ithaca, NY: Cornell University Press.

Shaxon, Nicholas. 2011. *Treasure Islands: Tax Havens and the Men Who Stole the World*. London: Vintage.

Srnicek, Nick. 2017. *Platform Capitalism*. Cambridge: Polity.

Stockhammer, Englebert. 2010. *Financialization and the Global Economy*. PERI Working Paper 240. Amherst, MA: PERI.

Sudarsanam, Sudi. 1995. *The Essence of Mergers and Acquisitions*. London: Prentice Hall.

Sunday Times. 2017. *Sunday Times Rich List*. Special insert, May 7.

UBS-PwC. 2017. *Billionaires Report*. London: UBS-PwC.

Useem, Michael. 1984. *The Inner Circle: Large Corporations and the Rise of Political Activity in the US and UK*. Oxford: Oxford University Press.

Wedel, Janine. 2014. *Unaccountable*. New York: Pegasus Books.

Wilkinson, Richard, and Kate Pickett. 2010. *The Spirit Level: Why Equality Is Better for Everyone*. London: Penguin.

Wilks-Heeg, Stuart, Andrew Blick, and Stephen Crone. 2012. *How Democratic Is the UK: The 2012 Audit*. Liverpool: Democratic Audit.

Aeron Davis is professor of political communication and codirector of the Political Economy Research Centre at Goldsmiths, University of London. His research ranges across political communication, economic sociology, media and communication, and elite studies. He is the author of five books and two edited collections, including, most recently, *Reckless Opportunists: Elites at the End of the Establishment* (2018).

RUSSIAN PHILANTHROCAPITALISM

Elisabeth Schimpfössl

Abstract This article investigates philanthropic practices among Russia's hyper-rich. It ponders whether and to what extent philanthrocapitalist concepts are compatible with traditional Russian approaches to elite philanthropy, which have been shaped and controlled by the country's domineering state. Some of the multimillionaires and billionaires interviewed for this research have married philanthrocapitalist ideas with beliefs molded by their Soviet past and their self-perception as belonging to the intelligentsia. Such distinct and seemingly morally superior identities, together with active engagement in philanthropy, act as a lever with which to foster trust in the new social hierarchies and legitimize them across generations.

Keywords billionaires, charity, philanthropy, Russia, elite, legitimacy

Delving into the world of Russia's hyper-rich, this article investigates the historical and cultural features of their philanthropic practices and asks to what extent they are compatible with the idea of philanthrocapitalism. Such a research agenda raises several issues: First, these mega-rich individuals are striving to justify their fortunes in a society where, not so long ago, wealth was considered a crime and where today the gap between rich and poor has grown to become one of the widest in the world. Second, philanthrocapitalism is, by design, the antithesis to Russia's history of philanthropy, which has always existed within the control of a highly centralized state. Third, the new wealthy elite in Russia lacks the birthright of a capitalist class that was brought up with bourgeois values and had a sense of duty and entitlement instilled into them.

105

Cultural Politics, Volume 15, Issue 1, © 2019 Duke University Press
DOI: 10.1215/17432197-7289556

This is highly problematic: as Max Weber reiterated, the holders of power and wealth want to believe that they deserve their good fortunes because of who they are and what they constitute (1991: 271). With the first generation of Russia's hyper-rich having cemented their wealth, it has become more important to them to feel that they deserve the positions they occupy and the benefits they have accrued. As a consequence of this change in priorities, social responsibility has become obligatory, resulting in a rapid rise in charitable giving in the new millennium. Philanthropy is particularly important for the older upper-class members, who have begun to think about the legacy they will leave after their death.

All this was not an issue in the early post-Soviet period. The 1990s were dominated by the extreme prestige of money, no matter how it was acquired. Now that they have emancipated themselves from the urge to make more money, they have the freedom to ponder their cultural and spiritual identities—one of the luxuries that Pierre Bourdieu (1984) described as the privilege of being rich. Accordingly, upper-class Russians have sought to engage in more intellectual activities and display more cultured traits. However, they lack the cultural templates of a bourgeois predecessor and rely instead on the Russian intelligentsia, whose values were filtered through the Soviet experience (Schimpfössl 2018: 97, 83). As I argue in this article, this legacy is to a large extent compatible with philanthrocapitalist ideas.

Defining Philanthrocapitalism and Elite Philanthropy

The term *philanthrocapitalism* stems from Matthew Bishop's and Michael Green's *Philanthrocapitalism: How the Rich Can Save the World and Why We Should Let* *Them* (2008). The foreword to the book was written by Bill Clinton, whose foundation trades as a model example of philanthrocapitalism, as do the Bill and Melinda Gates Foundation and the Chan Zuckerberg Initiative. The concept postulates that the application of for-profit business methods in philanthropy is superior to traditional public-sector or civil-society approaches and has a substantially greater impact on social change. Philanthrocapitalism is also applied to venture capitalists, social investors and entrepreneurs, who believe that their business activities stimulate the wider social good on a global scale. Advocates of philanthrocapitalism devote a lot of attention to measuring the impact of their work. They also leverage money other than their own, primarily from governments.

Many scholars and commentators have fundamentally questioned the positive impact of this supposedly innovative approach to philanthropy. Linsey McGoey (2012: 186–89) does not see anything new about philanthrocapitalism: for over a century, philanthropists have sought to model philanthropic giving on corporate practices; conflating the market economy's benefits for the common good was already part of Adam Smith's *Wealth of Nations*. The one thing that McGoey recognizes as truly new is the previously unseen level to which philanthrocapitalists are happy to admit how financially lucrative such an approach can be with regard to their business (193).

More importantly, critics argue that large-scale giving has corrosive effects on democracy (Edwards 2010; McGoey 2015; Callahan 2017; Reich 2018). Philanthropists are not elected by anybody and, hence, not accountable to anyone but themselves. They pursue their individual policy agendas, without being able to foresee the consequences, even though their choices may affect millions of people. Philanthropic choices might well counteract those of the public as to how to allocate funds (Reich 2018: 10). Tax reductions for philanthropy deprive state treasuries of resources which could otherwise be used for social welfare and public infrastructure. The deleterious effect on democracy is particularly stark where taxpayers' money is used to match private donations.

In contrast to such a macro-level critique, sociologists of elites typically explore philanthropy from a perspective of elite legitimation and reproduction. One of the most seminal studies in this tradition is *Why the Wealthy Give* by Francie Ostrower (1995), who explored the elite culture of affluent donors in New York City.[1] Ostrower paid particular attention to her wealthy respondents' class identity and how they use philanthropy to promote an elitist way of life. This understanding of elite philanthropy is central to this article because it outlines the specifics of philanthropy as a means to gain legitimacy, secure and control class boundaries, and perpetuate social positions across generations.

Philanthropy has been defined in many different ways, and there are long debates as to how it relates to charity. I draw on Ostrower's definition of philanthropy, which includes charity and patronage as well as alms giving and the encouragement of self-help (1995: 4, 20). In her understanding, charity is specifically directed toward the poor, whereas philanthropy has broader aims and objectives. The latter does include charity, but it also encompasses the wider practices of private giving to the arts, environmental causes, health and rehabilitation, education, universities, museums, religious organizations, parks, cultural institutions, youth, and urban development.

Empirical Data

The material analyzed in this article is drawn from a set of eighty interviews with entrepreneurs and their spouses or children, which I conducted between 2008 and 2017, mostly in Moscow. Their characteristics are typical of the post-Soviet elite, the most salient of which is that they are highly educated (Kryshtanovskaia 2004: 341–42). For this article I selected twelve interviewees, eight men and four women. They all are philanthropists and run their own foundation or charity (many of them parallel to their corporate foundations) or were cofounders of a foundation and have since been heavily involved. The eight men are the breadwinners in their families. Three of the four women are the wives of wealthy Russian men; the fourth is a sibling. Except for one couple, whom I interviewed in 2009, these selected interviews took place between 2015 and 2017.

The two earlier interviews, which took place in 2009, were with Maria Eliseeva and Ilia Segalovich, the cofounder of Yandex, the world's fourth largest search engine and Russia's equivalent to Google. Segalovich died from cancer in 2013, not having reached the age of fifty. His wife, Eliseeva, set up her charity Deti Marii (Maria's Children) in the early 1990s, and both were active in running its activities.

Veronika Zonabend is married to Ruben Vardanian, born in 1968 and former CEO and controlling shareholder of Troika Dialog, an investment bank. His assets were worth $950 million in 2017.[2] Through their foundation, Initiatives for Development of Armenia, they run an international boarding school, United World College Dilijan in Armenia, which Veronika looks after. Her husband is heavily involved in the development of Skolkovo Moscow School of Management, which he cofounded and where a research center was created in

2013 for the study of philanthropy, social entrepreneurship, and ways to pass down assets from the first generation of wealthy people in Russia to the next.

Irina Sedykh is the wife of the metallurgy tycoon Anatolii Sedykh, the main shareholder of United Metallurgical Company (OMK), Russia's second-largest pipe producer and biggest manufacturer of train wheels. He is also the president of the OMK-Uchastie (OMK-Participation) Charity Fund, which focuses on education, health, and children with special needs. Irina Sedykh chairs the fund's supervisory board and is heavily involved in its activities.

The fourth woman is Irina Prokhorova, born in 1956 and the sister of Mikhail Prokhorov, who was born in 1965 and topped Russia's rich list in 2009 with assets of $22.6 billion (down to $8.9 billion in 2017). Prokhorova is the founder of *New Literary Observer*, the main intellectual journal and publishing house in Russia. She leads a philanthropic foundation named after her brother.

Piotr Aven, born in 1955, is chairman of Russia's biggest private bank, Alfa-Bank. In 2016 his assets were worth $4.6 billion. He is cofounder of Liniia Zhizni (Life Line), a charity that organizes surgeries for children, and of Genesis Philanthropy Group, which supports Russian-speaking Jews worldwide. Aven regularly lends pieces of his art collections to museums. He is a trustee of several museums and universities.

Vadim Moshkovich, born in 1967, is the head of the agro-industrial holding company Rusagro, Russia's largest sugar and pork producer. In 2016 his assets amounted to $2.3 billion. His main philanthropic activity is the development of a flagship school for highly gifted children. Fifty million dollars of his private money has gone into the project, and $150 million

into an endowment fund that will help keep things running.

Alexander Svetakov, born in 1963, also specializes in schools; however, in contrast to Moshkovich's school, these schools are for disabled children. Svetakov is the owner of Absolut Group, which has interests in real estate, trading, and insurance. His assets amount to $3.3 billion in 2017.

Roman Avdeev, born in 1967, owns Moscow Credit Bank, one of Russia's most significant in terms of assets. His wealth in 2014 was assessed at $1.4 billion. He runs a foundation working with orphans and foster parents.

Ziyavudin Magomedov, also born in 1967, is the main owner of Summa Group, which invests in port logistics, engineering, construction, telecommunications, and oil and gas. His wealth amounted to $1.4 billion in 2014. His PERI Charitable Foundation largely works in Dagestan, his country of birth; however, their financing might dry up soon. Magomedov was about to fly to the United States with his family in late March 2018 when he and his brother were arrested and charged with setting up an organized crime group and embezzling state funds. On May 30 the court extended the arrest until August 5. In the very worst-case scenario, Magomedov could be handed down a prison sentence of thirty years (Starinskaia 2018).

The remaining two interviewees are not billionaires. How rich they are is difficult to tell. Igor Tsukanov, born in 1962, is a former financier and the only one who permanently lives in London. He has never publicly given a price tag to his wealth. His collection of postwar Russian art is one of the largest in the world. He organizes his various philanthropic projects through the Tsukanov Family Foundation. Oleg Sysuev, born in 1953, is an Alfa-Bank board member. In the 1990s, he was deputy head of the presidential administration, the government's vice prime minister, and minister of labor. Sysuev is a founding member of Liniia Zhizni, together with Piotr Aven and others.

Philanthrocapitalist Ideas among Russia's Hyper-Rich

The current generation of hyper-rich grew up on Soviet propaganda, which taught them that the capitalist system inevitably spawns gains for a few to the detriment of the masses. Reality in the 1990s very much confirmed this Soviet propaganda take on capitalism: while the new wealthy elites speedily enriched themselves, the country's gross domestic product shrank by half, the population's living standards crumbled, and poverty exploded (Scheidel 2017: 222).

During the long oil boom of the 2000s, the memory of Soviet propaganda and the 1990s cut-throat capitalism faded. This allowed philanthrocapitalist ideas to be articulated. The oligarch Aven believes that the private sector will be supplanting the state and that private money will increasingly finance social infrastructure, covering everything from medicine to culture. He sees this as inherent in the logic of the market, stating, "Where capitalism develops, private philanthropy will emerge and grow." Aven considers a strengthening of philanthropy to be of particular importance to Russia, as this will help rehabilitate private property.

Liniia Zhizni, set up by the shareholders of Aven's bank, was the brainchild of the oligarch Mikhail Fridman. Sysuev, one of the shareholders, told me, "Misha [Mikhail] used his success in business and applied it to charity: business technology, good management, motivated with clear tasks, audit, and control." Sysuev pondered the weaknesses of this approach:

"What we don't have enough of are those emotional drivers, enticed by the soul," he admitted. "But maybe that's also good. We don't give money if we can't control it to the end."

According to the former financier Igor Tsukanov, successful businesspeople know best how to achieve a particular result, how to do a project, and how to organize a big event. They can easily switch from one project to another, and they can apply their skills to any field, not just business. After Tsukanov stopped doing business, he wanted to do something new: "But the new thing had to have parameters: clear objectives, a time frame, and a budget. These are the skills I acquired in business and applied to art." He regards his own philanthropy as highly structured and is very happy with what he is doing; he is now one of the world's leading collectors of postwar Russian art: "Exhibitions require efforts, logistics, and intellectual input. They are large projects."

Other interviewees did not articulate philanthrocapitalist ideas that explicitly, but there were elements of it. Zonabend, who calls herself and her husband, Vardanian, social entrepreneurs, relates to philanthropy in the same way she relates to the market. They were among the first who started "helping systematically. . . . You need a system, otherwise there is no impact, and this system needs to be sustainable in the long run." Magomedov's foundation runs an innovation business incubator to develop entrepreneurial IT technology skills among young people in Dagestan. In his project, Moshkovich wants "to have the goals clearly defined and to understand how to get there, how to measure success, etc." He is concerned about producing graduates whose skill set can compete with the West.

Philanthrocapitalism promotes the

idea that competitive principles epitomize freedom of choice and individualism. The desire to express individualism and to experience this freedom of choice has a paradoxical consequence in Russia: people barely differ in their approaches. The vast majority of charity donors support children, and giving aid to children is the major form of charity in Russia (Khodorova 2014; Skolkovo 2015: 78, 81). This is, first, because only children are considered trustworthy in a society that is largely based on distrust (Hosking 2014). Second, support for children is an investment in the future of Russia, an issue the new upper class has become increasingly concerned about. Third, support for children follows the Russian tradition of charity that emphasizes benevolence toward passive alms takers (Dinello 1998).

Michael Edwards (2008) cautions that competitive principles should be applied to the third sector. They are likely to push nonprofits to economize in key areas of their work, eschew the most complicated and expensive issues, and avoid those most difficult to reach. In a pure form, competitive principles inevitably exclude care for groups with little "use" for society. This is, however, not the main reason Russian philanthropists are little concerned about groups other than children, such as migrants, homeless people, drug addicts, ex-prisoners, or the long-term unemployed. Here near–social Darwinist attitudes, which were prevalent in the dog-eat-dog world of the 1990s, prevail: those who can work should do so and earn their own living, and those who are considered to have caused their own misery are not deserving of mercy (Schimpfössl 2018: 110).

The State and Philanthropy in Russian History

Nascent philanthrocapitalist ideas are confronted by an intrusive Russian state. In this respect, historically in Russia, there is very little ground for philanthrocapitalists to build on. Philanthropy was initially confined to the aristocracy and the monarchy. The tsars kept tight control over who was allowed to give and to whom. At the same time they were showing largesse themselves, as well as permitting the ladies of the court to keep themselves occupied with philanthropic giving. The results were a great number of educational and healthcare institutions as well as institutions of art and culture (Khodorova 2014). An example of this is the State Hermitage, based on the collection of Catherine the Great, which opened to the public in 1852. By the mid- to late nineteenth century, when Russia's industrialization took on pace, industrialists, financiers, and merchants accumulated sufficient wealth to divert some of it to charitable causes. This philanthropy covered a wide range of areas, from cultural institutions and the arts to social trusteeships or social welfare (Dinello 1998: 117–19). This period is most strongly imprinted in today's philanthropists' minds. Zonabend told me that prior to the First World War 50 percent of all educational institutions were funded by benefactors, and Christian schools were all privately funded by money from the community, the church, and private individuals: "The rich felt a duty to support the development of their country." She evaluated their giving very positively, relating it back to the nature of the state: "It has always been like this here. We have always had a heavy bureaucracy with people at the top who have never particularly cared about the well-being of their people. So the responsibility to care about the country and its people fell to the rich." Moving on to the 1917 Revolution, Zonabend deplored that this feeling of duty was lost as a result. Even worse, "many philanthropists of that time supported the revolutionaries."

Under Soviet rule, the authorities fully institutionalized social welfare and forbade all philanthropic activities. They perceived them as a capitalist practice that undermined the role of the Communist Party (Kurilla 2002). Philanthropy lived on, however, operating under different terms. High-ranking party members patronized the arts even in the toughest of all times, the 1930s (Fitzpatrick 2015). In the postwar Soviet Union, charity was routinely provided through the various Communist Party organizations (Dinello 1998: 115). Some of my interviewees, such as Segalovich, remembered those disguised charity activities very clearly, as well as their own commitment to them when visiting orphanages and the like.

In the early 1990s, a small number of Russia's new businessmen pursued philanthropic activities, but they were usually sporadic, unfocused, and uncoordinated. The population dismissed them as PR stunts as well as attempts of the new rich to soothe a guilty conscience and schmooze with the authorities (Gambrell 2004). After the economy had recovered from the 1998 financial crisis, charity rose rapidly (Khodorova 2014). An increasing number of businesses began institutionalizing their corporate philanthropy programs through corporate foundations. Major shareholders sometimes played a key role in this. Russian companies also began to embrace the notion of corporate social responsibility (Coutts 2014). This was influenced in part by intensified encounters

with their Western counterparts and in part by Vladimir Putin. Frequently using the term *social responsibility*, Putin made it clear early in his presidency that he expected those who accrued a certain level of wealth to help fill the vacuum left by the withdrawal of the state. His encouragements had their intended effect. In 2006 almost 90 percent of donations in Russia went to state-run bodies financing health care, nursing homes, orphanages, and cultural institutions, thereby stepping in where the state had failed (Livshin and Weitz 2006).

Cynics regard such philanthropic efforts as pay-offs to remain in Putin's good books. Roman Abramovich was famously obliged to pump large sums into Chukotka, a remote region in the Far East he had no previous link to but that he represented for years in the Federation Council, the Russian upper house. Some equally doubt that Magomedov's interest in Dagestan, where he grew up, was primarily driven by care and compassion, rather than being a "necessary evil for winning favor with the Kremlin," which is keen to see Islamic extremism in the region contained (Dzutsati 2014).

In 1999 Vladimir Potanin, the wealthiest Russian in 2015, created the first private foundation, named after him. Since then, the number of private foundations has grown steadily. As of 2013, there were around seventy of them in Russia, many of which are endowed by their founders (Coutts 2014). These private organizations have been established parallel to corporate ones, and some philanthropists channel their personal philanthropy through their business. Most of them want to have full control over their activities, which is one reason why many foundations implement projects directly, as opposed to allocating grants to intermediary organizations, usually nongovernmental organizations (NGOs).

Another reason is that the NGO sector in Russia is seen as corrupt, fraudulent, and incompetent (Livshin and Weitz 2006; Khodorova 2014: 19; Skolkovo 2015: 78, 81, 83). In the aftermath of the 2004 Orange Revolution in Ukraine, Putin accused foreign NGOs (among them Amnesty International) of being instruments of foreign influence, secretly undermining Russia's interests. The introduction of two laws specifically targeting NGOs—the "foreign agent" law of July 2012 and the "undesirable organizations" law of May 2015—weakened the sector further. While attacking the NGO sector, the government introduced a more favorable environment for private philanthropists (Coutts 2014). In 2007 an endowment law was passed that made the income earned from endowments tax free. In 2012 tax incentives were introduced for individual donors. Kremlin-loyal NGOs have gained in strength and prestige (Robertson 2009).

In many Western countries, philanthropists tend to give globally as well as in the area they are economically active, or in the neighborhood where they grew up (Freeland 2013: 73–74; Lloyd 2004: 55). Patriotism is an important feature of their giving, and Russian philanthropists focus almost exclusively on Russia. Within the country, there too are geographic peculiarities. As Russia's hyper-rich are keen to control their giving and most of them live in Moscow, donations and philanthropic activities are concentrated in the capital and its surroundings (Coutts 2014). Parallel to this, natural resources are sourced from often very remote areas, and a lot of Russia's heavy industry is either energy based

or otherwise regionally concentrated. Most of these industrial centers were developed in late imperial Russia and Soviet times. In both periods, the state played the most crucial role in industrializing the country (Blackwell 1974).

When after the 1990s privatizations the oligarchs-to-be took over large industries left by the Soviet state, many of them ended up as the main employers in the region or town where their production, mines, or oilrigs were located. A crumbling social infrastructure, exacerbated by low wages and mass layoffs, caused severe social grievances. While not officially falling under the new owners' responsibilities, the highly desolate conditions in many regions nevertheless threatened to tarnish their image. In response, many corporations set up their foundations in the areas where their factories are located—and, thereby, filled some of the gaps in the underfunded public infrastructure. Opened in 2004, the Mikhail Prokhorov Foundation, run by Irina Prokhorova, focuses its work around the Siberian city Krasnoyarsk, where the oligarch's business is located. Theater productions and cultural activities feature prominently in the foundation's program. Anatolii Sedykh has his main production in Vyksa, a town in the Nizhny Novgorod region. His foundation, led by his wife Irina, aims at "unifying the company's work on a social level." She also organizes an annual cultural festival in the town.

Prokhorova's and Sekykh's commitment to cultural development is somewhat reminiscent of the mission that Russian intellectuals—many of them from aristocratic backgrounds—pursued in the second half of the nineteenth century when they tried to teach the peasantry how to achieve a better life, some with a degree of paternalism, others with an enlightenment mission (Schimpfössl 2018: 106). "We want to unite people and encourage them to take part in other people's life," Sedykh said. She sees this as "a way of helping develop civil society." Practically, this works via "volunteer participation" in the provision of care for disabled children. It has taken off, she said; every year there are more volunteers than the charity can reasonably integrate into its work.

In theory, strong state dominance, which heavily interferes in individual and corporate philanthropy, is incompatible with the concept of philanthrocapitalism. In Russia, however, philanthrocapitalism and a strong state can coexist harmoniously, as long as philanthropists accept the "rules of the game" dictated by the authorities. "Sure, many things are not quite clear here. That's something one needs to simply accept," Zonabend said. "But the state is not interfering," she insisted. "In sum, there are great chances here. We have much fewer restrictions than you have in Europe."

Educating and Enlightening
the Russian People

The prospect of a return on investment has never crossed some of my interviewees' minds. Eliseeva's protégés would have little chance otherwise. They are from disadvantaged backgrounds, many with severe learning difficulties, some mentally disabled. She wants to enable them to develop skills by making them enjoy learning: "We paint together, we have music classes, theatre classes, clown classes, and so on." Older ones can attend evening classes: Spanish, Italian, English, literature, and math. "You need to deal with these kids and challenge them; then everything will be very different." Many people think

that these children will never be able to read or write, but Eliseeva and her husband proved them wrong, as he told me: "Some of them even make it into college."

Market-oriented thinking would not allow for Avdeev's activities or Svetakov's school either. Avdeev, a father of twenty-three, nineteen of whom were adopted, sees the key to improving the lives of orphans in winning the hearts of people able and potentially willing to foster children. There is not much financial gain in setting up a school for children with mental impediments, as did Svetakov; neither is there much appetite in Russia for a project of this kind, as he explained to me: "Our society likes the strong and healthy. It doesn't like the weak and infirm." Many of the children in his school are physically disabled or the children of alcoholics. "It's not something many are comfortable with, you know," he said. Friends in politics and business tried to talk him out of his project: why not a school for gifted children, they asked.

A school for gifted children is what Moshkovich set up. Within a new development project, he was contractually obliged to build fifty schools. As he sees schools as being crucial to "shape human beings (and all humans are able to be good)," he decided that, as he has to build schools anyway, he would build only good schools: "A strong school is easily explained: it's an institution which not only teaches a child professional knowledge, competences, skills, morals, but has them undergo a complex development with clearly set goals." Moshkovich, who went to an elite school specializing in mathematics, believes that he owes his success in good part to his school education. (This is one reason he describes himself as "Soviet—I'm a product of the Soviet period.") Tsukanov went to the same school. He is also convinced that his education was excellent: "I don't know why the communists did that, but they did." Also in broader terms, he acknowledged the educational spirit in the Soviet Union, especially among educated families: "We had a big library at home and I grew up on books. It's a typical Soviet story. We had nothing else except education and books." Magomedov, who strongly identifies with his parents' intelligentsia status, was convinced that his Dagestan school program would prosper as it builds on the Soviet legacy of investing generously in education.

Most of my interviewees were born into the Soviet intelligentsia, which consisted of professionals engaged in the cultural and educational sector as well as academically trained medics, technicians, and engineers. By the time of Joseph Stalin's purges, the Soviet intelligentsia had largely lost their predecessors' ideals of a humanistic search for truth and a self-effacing devotion to serving the people (Hamburg 2010). What they retained was a strong patriotic feeling of duty to the state, as well as the nineteenth-century perception of society being divided into two classes: the educated intelligentsia and the simple masses (Berlin 2008: 130–54). The former repeatedly went out to lift the latter from their ignorance and poverty, seemingly selflessly, as did, for example, the Narodniks in the 1870s. Today many upper-class Russians embrace the intelligentsia as a group on whom to model themselves (Schimpfössl 2018: 97). This has been one of the drivers for the new economic elite to distance themselves from the ostentatious lifestyles they used to indulge in and to identify more with cultural symbols (Schimpfössl 2014). Such

attitudes reverberate in the interviewees' calling—to enlighten the people. Some of my interviewees fancy themselves as moral leaders.

A self-perception as moral leaders is not necessarily in disagreement with a philanthrocapitalist philosophy. Sysuev sees his duty in enlightening and educating common Russian people so as to create "the social institute of charity" in Russia. Ordinary people should develop a need to do charity like "an everyday thing." The shareholders finance the charity's infrastructure and staff costs. The staff's main task is to fund-raise among common people for the surgery and treatment of severely ill children. In this way, the shareholders believe, they can instill in the people a desire to make charity part of their lives; thus they will become part of civil society. The shareholders' end goal is, however, more ambitious: to "rehabilitate private property in Russia." Sysuev explained: "The relationship to rich people is complex here in Russia. There is still the widespread belief that big money is stolen." This was also the reason the shareholders kept their involvement secret for many years. They feared that it could jeopardize the whole project.

Social Reproduction

In one respect philanthrocapitalism cannot possibly claim to make any difference when compared to previous philanthropic endeavors: its effect on legitimizing and re-creating social class. Nevertheless, advocates of philanthrocapitalism evaluate this positively; great riches generate extra money, and this extra money can be invested into social projects. Furthermore, social status obliges and nurtures a feeling of duty. This is something that scholars scrutinizing elite culture have widely written about, among them famously Georg Simmel ([1908] 1992: 820) in his elaboration of noblesse oblige.

However personally motivated their giving may seem, in fact, it is often highly regulated through formal and informal rules. The elite is sensitive to questions such as who gives to whom, who is allowed to give, and who is allowed to receive. In the West, elite philanthropy is strongly related to being accepted by and identified with long-established, highly prestigious nonprofit organizations. Becoming a trustee of one of these indicates that one has socially "arrived" (Ostrower 1995: 36). In Russia, similar principles apply; however, they are realized through informal practices based on personal relations of trust. Whether formal or informal, such practices play the role of a social catalyst guarding the boundaries of social class and deciding who belongs to which elitist circles. Within these circles, very much in line with Marcel Mauss's observations ([1898] 2002), interdependence and social obligations are created and re-created.

Apart from the bonding among upper-class peers, philanthropy is also one of the most important tools to create a lasting legacy of cross-generational wealth. The first generation of wealth in Russia is growing older and their members are coming closer to death. The assets they will pass on to their offspring are on an epic scale; we will soon see one of the biggest transfers of wealth the world has ever seen, particularly if one considers the small number of people involved (Schimpfössl 2018: 150). Against this backdrop, a certain training in philanthropy has become an integral part of what is considered a proper upbringing. Many children of the hyper-rich are on track to acquire legitimacy.

Avdeev would be delighted if his children continued his legacy by running his foundation, but, like many others, he stressed that this should be of their own volition. "It's much more important to me that they live their own lives," he said. "The older they get, the less I try to give them advice. An older child has a right to make his or her own decisions and make their own mistakes." Avdeev's children will have plenty of chance to do so. He does not intend to bequeath his wealth to any of them. What they receive is high-quality education, accommodation, and a car.

Zonabend and her husband also say they will not pass on their wealth to their children. Moshkovich and Svetakov intend to strictly regulate the amount their children will receive, while large parts of their fortunes will go to charity. Being deprived of a windfall inheritance is likely to enable the children to find a place in society that will make them appear deserving in their own right, regardless of the fact that they were born into privilege.

Social Inequality

Philanthrocapitalism has become fashionable at a time of increasing social inequality, with the wealth of a tiny group of hyper-rich multiplying exponentially. Never before in history has social inequality widened as rapidly as it has in Russia since the collapse of the Soviet Union (Scheidel 2017: 222; Therborn 2013: 8). In 2013 Credit Suisse declared Russia as one of the countries with the highest level of wealth inequality in the world (Keating et al. 2013: 53). The plunge in oil prices in 2014 undermined many of the gains made in the living standards of ordinary Russians during the early 2000s (Pirani 2010: 10; Tikhonova and Mareeva 2016: 162). However, rich Russians have barely felt the consequences of either the 2008 or the 2014 crises; the number of dollar billionaires recovered quickly (*Forbes Russia* 2017).

Svetakov sometimes has difficulties understanding his less fortunate fellow Russians: "Our people are particular. They've had everything taken away, but they still endure it." That should not cause him sleepless nights, others say. "The population has become a lot richer in the last twenty, thirty years," Aven insisted. He admitted that there is a problem of income inequality (which, shockingly to him, is already as high as in the United States, he added), but "the group of very rich people is very small and they live separately from the rest." As for tackling the problem of inequality, he sees the responsibility lying with the state: "It's a question of social policy. Social mobility must work. There mustn't be any nepotism." He assured me that there is certainly not any risk "whatsoever" of social protests erupting in Russia.

Industrialists closely involved in day-to-day business are the most likely to face moral dilemmas. Anatolii Sedykh reduced his staff after the 2014 crisis hit. His wife told me that even up to the eleventh hour they tried to save their business projects, whether profitable or not. Their foundation tried to mitigate the consequences of these layoffs, she assured me. Moshkovich too seemed at loggerheads with the basic demands of capitalism and his own role in it: "I'm not a politician, I'm a small person. I don't deal with inequality. I don't care about inequality," he said. The issue, however, does bother him "in an empirical sense, in cases where I encounter it." His company employs fifteen thousand people. He noted: "When we increase productivity, this means mass redundancies. . . . We need to sack people all the time." Even

though he is not personally involved in any such executive processes, they clearly make him feel uneasy; after all, they clash with his idea of being responsible toward his workers, and his desire to secure them a decent life. ("We build houses for our employees, raise their wages, educate their children, and so on.")

Critics of philanthropy, such as Edwards (2008), argue that governments achieved far more over the last century through implementing social programs, especially when pressurized by social movements and civil society. Avdeev might partly agree with that. He thinks that "rich people can only contribute with their ideas"; however, "the main discussion needs to run in civil society." In general, Avdeev allots an important role to the people, a view that originates from his Soviet values. "The April theses? Bread to all?" he asked me. "How could one possibly not agree with that?" He then told me that he appreciates Vladimir Lenin, not least for his qualities as a gifted propagandist and journalist. Avdeev embraces Marxist ideas in general; "although there is a lot of utopia in Marx. Then again, utopian ideas are not only bad after all." Eventually, Avdeev lamented that one crucial demand put forward by Karl Marx has not been implemented: the abolition of inheritance.

Conclusion

Attempts undertaken by the hyper-rich to legitimize themselves through philanthropy help strengthen ties between them and facilitate cohesion among the various elite groups. Zonabend and Vardanian are in many respects spearheading Russia's new upper class. Their class consciousness is highly developed, witnessed not only by ensuring their children acquire high status, but by setting up an institution to coach Russia's rich how to pass down wealth to their offspring in a sustainable way. As for their intrafamily reproduction, Zonabend and Vardanyan have gone one stop further by pledging to disinherit their children and give their money to charity instead. This is, in fact, the biggest favor parents can grant their children to give them legitimacy. It is the most powerful and impressive way the super-wealthy have to remove the stigma their children carry of being born with a silver spoon in their mouth.

The same is true for Aven and Sysuev. McGoey grants philanthrocapitalism a genuine novelty: the level to which bene-factors are open about the fact that their charity enhances their business prospects (2012: 194). Albeit as part of a long-term perspective, Aven's and Sysuev's invest-ment in charity has as its aim the rehabil-itation of the status of private property in Russia; and this obviously entwines with their own interest. Yet again, as with Var-danian, they pursue not only their personal self-interest but also the interest of their class as a whole.

A factor that has greatly facilitated their (self-)legitimization is their intelli-gentsia identity, and this echoes in their philanthropic practices. Although to varying extents, Zonabend, Vardanian, Aven, and Sysuev presented themselves as educators who see their duty in teach-ing their common fellow citizens civil soci-ety values. The credibility of moral lead-ership benefits from historically founded status—birthright and entitlement—and this is what they claim for themselves, among other things, by emphasizing their intelligentsia background.

There is, of course, a factor that damp-ens such efforts to assume moral leader-ship: the radical economic transformation in the 1990s, which was the precondition of my interviewees' riches. It could only acquire such a radical form because there

was no significant force in society willing or able to contest the changes under way. This course of events was warmly wel-comed by not only the liberal reformers in Russia but also their Western advisors, many of whom deplore the lack of a civil society in Russia today (Domrin 2003: 31n; Uhlin 2006: 163). None of my interviewees delved into this, which is interesting in itself. It indicates that Russia's new upper class has not yet found an entirely con-vincing narrative about the origin of their money, which they today so generously give to charity.

All this does not necessarily make Russia's hyper-rich unsuitable for philan-throcapitalism if it is understood not as an ideological idea but as a practical tool to justify wealth inequality. Arguing that private and corporate surplus money is the necessary precondition that sets free resources for philanthropy, however, has its own drawback: On the one hand, Sveta-kov and Eliseeva would not be able to run their projects for mentally disabled or oth-erwise disadvantaged children were it not for their riches. On the other hand, their projects would not exist if they reasoned purely in philanthrocapitalist terms. Their involvement with severely disadvantaged children does not fit into categories such as impact-oriented, measurable, result based, market savvy, high performing, cost effective, or financially profitable.

My interviewees were all born in the Soviet Union, most of them in the Bre-zhnev era. Their Soviet upbringing and education forms a major part of their iden-tity. If they refuted their past, this would mean denying, to some extent, their own worthiness. This creates some conflicting ideas in terms of how they comprehend their role in the system and the new social hierarchy. This conflict is particularly appar-ent in Moshkovich, who perceives himself

Elisabeth Schimpfössl

as a product of Soviet society, and Avdeev, who identifies with the ideological concepts that founded the Soviet project. As little related to philanthrocapitalism as such an analysis might sound, in a lighter and dampened version it has global parallels: the world's richest are increasingly borrowing some terminology traditionally ascribed to the socially caring, occasionally even the radical Left, when talking about their efforts to change the world and connect with the common people (*Forbes* 2012).

Such efforts naturally stop short of challenging the status quo with regard to wealth distribution. Increased philanthropic activities and, in particular, the current fashion of philanthrocapitalism reflect the power of individual money and its extreme concentration. These circumstances reinforce its influence, not least in relation to the state. This is also the explanation for why there is very little tension, if not full-on cooperation, between philanthrocapitalists and the state. This is true even for Russia. Sure, some of the rich resent having projects allocated to them by the authorities. However, once they submit to the game and play it right, Russia is full of opportunities for those well established within the power system. Merging philanthrocapitalist and Soviet ideologies is in many ways doing the trick—and, to a large extent, characterizes Russia's new upper class and the philanthropists among it.

Acknowledgments
I am grateful to the Leverhulme Trust for enabling this research through the award of a Leverhulme Early Career Fellowship.

Notes
1. This study served as a model for many others. It was replicated in the United Kingdom (albeit following a more practice-oriented concept) by Theresa Lloyd in 2004, with a follow-up she wrote together with Beth Breeze in 2013 (Breeze and Lloyd 2013).
2. All wealth indicators are taken from *Forbes Russia*.

References
Berlin, Isaiah. 2008. "The Remarkable Decade." In *Russian Thinkers*, edited by Henry Hardy and Aileen Kelly, 130–54. London: Penguin.

Bishop, Matthew, and Michael Green. 2008. *Philanthrocapitalism: How the Rich Can Save the World and Why We Should Let Them*. London: A. and C. Black.

Blackwell, W. L. 1974. *Russian Economic Development from Peter the Great to Stalin*. New York: Watts.

Bourdieu, Pierre. 1984. *Distinction: A Social Critique of the Judgment of Taste*. London: Routledge and Paul Kegan.

Breeze, Beth, and Theresa Lloyd. 2013. *Richer Lives: Why Rich People Give*. London: Directory of Social Change.

Callahan, David. 2017. *The Givers: Wealth, Power, and Philanthropy in a New Gilded Age*. New York: Knopf.

Coutts. 2014. *Million Dollar Donors Report 2014*. philanthropy.coutts.com/en/reports/2014/russia/findings.html.

Dinello, Natalia. 1998. "Philanthropy in Russia and the United States: Elites and Philanthropy in Russia." *International Journal of Politics, Culture, and Society* 12, no. 1: 109–33.

Domrin, Alexander N. 2003. "Ten Years Later: Society, 'Civil Society,' and the Russian State." *Russian Review* 62, no. 2: 193–211.

Dzutsati, Valery. 2014. "Kremlin Pushes Dagestani Billionaires to Invest in Dagestan." *Eurasia Daily Monitor* 11, no. 115. jamestown.org/program/kremlin-pushes-dagestani-billionaires-to-invest-in-dagestan-2/.

Edwards, Michael. 2008. "Philanthrocapitalism: After the Goldrush." *openDemocracy*, March 20. www.opendemocracy.net/node/36008/print.

Edwards, Michael. 2010. *Small Change: Why Business Won't Save the World*. San Francisco: Berrett-Koehler.

Fitzpatrick, Sheila. 2015. *On Stalin's Team: The Years of Living Dangerously in Soviet Politics*. Princeton, NJ: Princeton University Press.

Forbes. 2012. "The Forbes 400 Summit: Bill Gates, Warren Buffett, and the Greatest Roundtable of All Time." October 8. www.forbes.com/sites /randalllane/2012/09/18/the-forbes-400-summit -bill-gates-warren-buffett-and-the-greatest -roundtable-of-all-time/.

Forbes Russia. 2017. "200 Bogateishchikh biznesmenov Rossii 2017" ("200 Richest Businessmen in Russia in 2017"). April 20. www.forbes.ru /rating/342579–200-bogateyshih-biznesmenov -rossii-2017.

Freeland, Chrystia. 2013. *Plutocrats: The Rise of the New Global Super-Rich.* London: Penguin.

Gambrell, Jamey. 2004. "Philanthropy in Russia: New Money under Pressure." *Carnegie Reporter* 3, no. 1. www.carnegie.org/reporter/09/philanthropy /index.html.

Hamburg, Gary M. 2010. "Russian Intelligentsias." In *A History of Russian Thought*, edited by William Leatherbarrow and Derek Offord, 44–69. Cambridge: Cambridge University Press.

Hosking, Geoffrey. 2014. *Trust: A History.* Oxford: Oxford University Press.

Keating, Giles, Michael O'Sullivan, Anthony Shorrocks, James B. Davies, Rodrigo Lluberas, and Antonios Koutsoukis. 2013. *Global Wealth Report 2013.* Zurich: Credit Suisse.

Khodorova, Julia. 2014. *Russia Giving: Research on Individual Giving in Russia.* Moscow: Charity Aid Foundation Russia.

Kryshtanovskaia, Ol'ga. 2004. *Anatomiia Rossiiskoi elity* (*Anatomy of the Russian Elite*). Moscow: A. V.

Kurilla, Ivan. 2002. "Civil Activism without NGOs: The Communist Party as a Civil Society Substitute." *Demokratizatsiya: The Journal of Post-Soviet Democratization* 10, no. 3: 392–400.

Livshin, Alexander, and Richard Weitz. 2006. "Civil Society and Philanthropy under Putin." *International Journal of Not-for-Profit Law* 8, no. 3: 7–12.

Lloyd, Theresa. 2004. *Why Rich People Give.* London: Association of Charitable Foundations.

Mauss, Marcel. (1898) 2002. *The Gift: The Form and Reason for Exchange in Archaic Societies.* London: Routledge Classics.

McGoey, Linsey. 2012. "Philanthrocapitalism and Its Critics." *Poetics* 40, no. 2: 185–99.

McGoey, Linsey. 2015. *No Such Thing as a Free Gift: The Gates Foundation and the Price of Philanthropy.* London: Verso.

Ostrower, Francie. 1995. *Why the Wealthy Give: The Culture of Elite Philanthropy.* Princeton, NJ: Princeton University Press.

Pirani, Simon. 2010. *Change in Putin's Russia: Power, Money, and People.* London: Pluto.

Reich, Rob. 2018. *Just Giving: Why Philanthropy Is Failing Democracy and How It Can Do Better.* Princeton, NJ: Princeton University Press.

Robertson, Graeme B. 2009. "Managing Society: Protest, Civil Society, and Regime in Putin's Russia." *Slavic Review* 68, no. 3: 528–47.

Scheidel, Walter. 2017. *The Great Leveler: Violence and the History of Inequality from the Stone Age to the Twenty-First Century.* Princeton, NJ: Princeton University Press.

Schimpfössl, Elisabeth. 2014. "Russia's Social Upper Class: From Ostentation to Culturedness." *British Journal of Sociology* 65, no. 1: 63–81.

Schimpfössl, Elisabeth. 2018. *Rich Russians: From Oligarchs to Bourgeoisie.* New York: Oxford University Press.

Simmel, Georg. (1908) 1992. "Exkurs über den Adel" ("Excursus on the Nobility"). In *Soziologie: Untersuchungen über die Formen der Vergesellschaftung* (*Sociology: Inquiries into the Construction of Social Forms*), 816–31. Frankfurt: Suhrkamp.

Skolkovo Center for Management. 2015. *Issledovanie vladel'tsev kapitalov Rossii* (*Russia's Wealth Possessors Study*). Moscow: Center for Management, Wealth, and Philanthropy.

Starinskaia, Galina. 2018. "Vladel'tsy gruppy 'Summa' Ziiavudinu Magomedovu grozit do 30 let lisheniia svobody" ("The Owner of Summa Group, Ziiavudin Magomedov, Faces up to 30 Years in Prison"). *Vedomosti*, April 1. www.vedomosti .ru/business/articles/2018/04/02/755524 -ziyavudinu-magomedovu.

Therborn, Goran. 2013. *The Killing Fields of Inequality.* Cambridge: Polity.

Tikhonova, Natalya E., and Svetlana V. Mareeva. 2016. "Poverty in Contemporary Russian Society: Formation of a New Periphery." *Russian Politics* 1, no. 2: 159–83.

Elisabeth Schimpfössl

Uhlin, Anders. 2006. *Post-Soviet Civil Society: Democratisation in Russia and the Baltic States.* London: Routledge.

Weber, Max. 1991. *From Max Weber: Essays in Sociology.* Translated and edited by Hans Heinrich Gerth and C. Wright Mills. London: Routledge.

Elisabeth Schimpfössl is author of *Rich Russians: From Oligarchs to Bourgeoisie* (2018). Her current research focuses on elite philanthropy, both in Russia and the United Kingdom. She has also conducted research into media and journalism in Russia and Eastern Europe. Schimpfössl teaches social theory and media sociology at Aston University, Birmingham, where she is lecturer in sociology and policy.